500 CABINETS

500 CABINETS

A SHOWCASE OF DESIGN & CRAFTSMANSHIP

A Division of Sterling Publishing Co., Inc.
New York / London

SENIOR EDITOR
Ray Hemachandra

EDITOR
Julie Hale

ART DIRECTOR
Matt Shay

COVER DESIGNER
Kathy Holmes

FRONT COVER
Steven M. White
Yin, Yang, and Young | 2006
Photo by artist

SPINE
Jack Rodie
Za Zen | 2006
Photo by artist

BACK COVER, FROM TOP
Gregg Lipton
Three-Squared Cabinet | 2002
Photo by Dennis Griggs

Scott Grove
Amber | 2005
Photo by John Smillie

Jeremy Cox
Grid | 2007
Photo by artist

FRONT FLAP
Timothy Maddox
Naked Came the Weekend | 2007
Photo by Tim Barnwell

BACK FLAP
Jacob Knudsen
Negative Idea | 2004
Photo by Tyler Marshall

Library of Congress Cataloging-in-Publication Data

500 cabinets : a showcase of design & craftsmanship / author,
Ray Hemachandra -- 1st ed.
     p. cm.
  Includes index.
  ISBN 978-1-60059-575-2 (pb-pbk. with flaps : alk. paper)
  1. Case goods. 2. Artist-designed furniture. I. Title: Five hundred
cabinets. II. Title: Showcase of design & craftsmanship. III. Title:
Showcase of design and craftsmanship.
  NK2712.3.A15 2010
  749'.3--dc22

                                        2009046848

10 9 8 7 6 5 4 3 2 1

First Edition

Published by Lark Books, A Division of
Sterling Publishing Co., Inc.
387 Park Avenue South, New York, NY 10016

Text © 2010, Lark Book, A Division of Sterling Publishing Co., Inc.
Photography © 2010, Artist/Photographer

Distributed in Canada by Sterling Publishing,
c/o Canadian Manda Group, 165 Dufferin Street
Toronto, Ontario, Canada M6K 3H6

Distributed in the United Kingdom by GMC Distribution Services,
Castle Place, 166 High Street, Lewes, East Sussex, England BN7 1XU

Distributed in Australia by Capricorn Link (Australia) Pty Ltd.,
P.O. Box 704, Windsor, NSW 2756 Australia

If you have questions or comments about this book, please contact:
Lark Books
67 Broadway, Asheville, NC 28801
828-253-0467

Manufactured in China

ISBN 13: 978-1-60059-575-2

For information about custom editions, special sales, and premium
and corporate purchases, please contact the Sterling Special Sales
Department at 800-805-5489 or specialsales@sterlingpub.com.

For information about desk and examination copies available to college
and university professors, requests must be submitted to academic@
larkbooks.com. Our complete policy can be found at www.larkbooks.com.

Contents

Introduction

Kevin Irvin
Century Cabinet | 2006

In *A Cabinetmaker's Notebook*, James Krenov writes that "wood crafting is a combination of many things: discipline, a strong back, intuition, skilled fingers, something in the eye, and something more than professional skill." I kept this astute description in the back of my mind while serving as juror for *500 Cabinets* and let it guide me through the selection process. Choosing entries for this book was a challenging task, in part because most of the furniture that I created with my late wife, Carolyn Grew-Sheridan, was the result of an intuitive process. While we followed the functional requirements outlined by our customers, for the most part Carolyn and I trusted our instincts, creating proposals and finished pieces without putting forth any accompanying theories. Consequently, I sometimes find it difficult to articulate what makes furniture "great."

Krenov's words helped me formulate the criteria I needed for shaping this diverse collection—a book that reflects the variety of creative perspectives and high level of expertise that exists among woodworkers today. In addition to paying tribute to qualities like joinery, detailing, and color, *500 Cabinets* celebrates the wonderful contradictions that make furniture design such a vibrant medium. This book features a range of aesthetics, many of which work in delightful opposition to each other. Flip through these pages, and you'll notice the use of traditional as well as improbable materials, the application of cool logic and unbridled imagination, and a reliance on both balance and imbalance, harmony and tension. That furniture design has the capacity to embrace these opposites is a testament to its significance as a creative medium.

Whether through unique innovations in composition, subtle displays of craftsmanship, or bold conceptual approaches to design, today's furniture makers employ many different ways of making a statement. A number of artists included here emphasize structure by establishing strong contrasts between a cabinet's exterior and what it conceals. Joseph Walsh's *Collector's Cabinet*, Harold Shapiro's *Trident Cabinet*, and Fred Baier's *Time Capsule* are pieces with unassuming, modest facades that hide

interiors of puzzle-like complexity. Surface appearances to the contrary, their insides are sophisticated—full of clever cubbyholes, shelves, and compartments.

Other cabinets direct the viewer's attention to form through surprising details and sculptural approaches to construction. Jeff Johnson combines steel, mahogany, and glass in *Magnifying Cabinet*, an elegant, conceptual piece that on first glance could be taken

Dave Boykin
Cloud Buffet | 2008

for an art object. Dave Boykin's *Cloud Buffet* features shapely contours and beautifully figured wood, and Yuri Kobayashi's *Being*—an intricate wooden web—is a self-consciously complicated work.

Old-fashioned craftsmanship and precision remain touchstones for many contemporary furniture artists. Rooted in tradition, unembellished yet beautiful, Jeff Trigg's *Stereo Console*, Norman Pirollo's *Twin Plumes*, and Christopher Atwood's *Entertainment Console* are simply conceived cabinets that soar. The natural color and texture of the materials used—maple, cedar, and beech—shine through in these cabinets, and each piece has a handsome austerity that allows the purity of the design to speak for itself.

Other artists toy with the customary idea of what a cabinet is and use convention as a point of departure. Isaiah Schroeder's *Whiskey, You're the Devil*, which features a pitchfork handle and a pair of horns, is a wonderfully playful work, while John Eric Byers' *5 Ovals Dresser* and Kevin Irvin's *Century Cabinet* represent fresh twists on tradition. By playing outside the parameters—and playing with our fixed expectations about furniture—these artists give us new ways of looking at familiar forms.

Without a doubt, a successful piece of furniture must be driven by both material and concept, and the entries in *500 Cabinets* reflect this principle. Serving as juror for the book exposed me to a body of breathtaking work and awakened a new sense of excitement on my part regarding the future of furniture making. An ever-evolving medium with a long history, it remains rich with potential. As this collection proves, the possibilities for design seem limitless. Whether they cleave to tradition or reflect a visionary aesthetic, the cabinets and casework on these pages are all wonderful variations on a functional form. Look them over, and you're sure to view furniture in a new light.

John Grew Sheridan, juror

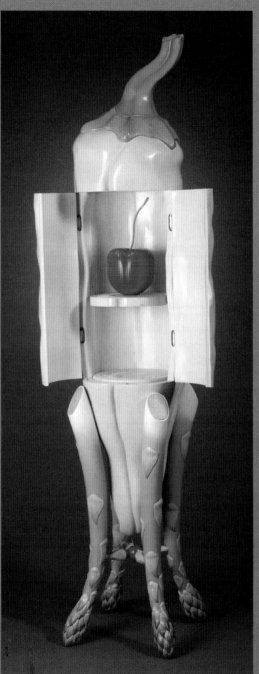

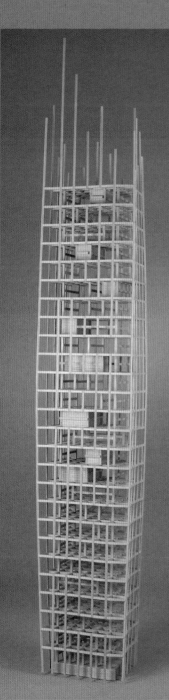
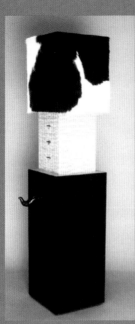

THE CABINETS

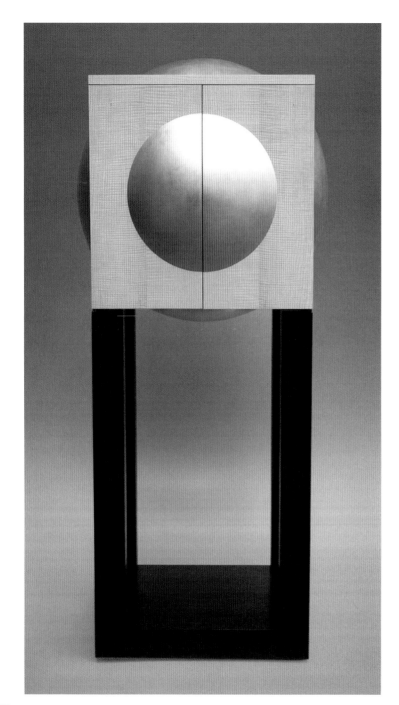

Taeyoul Ryu
Golden Gate | 2007
58 X 26 X 26 INCHES (147.3 X 66 X 66 CM)
Wenge, ash, maple, gold leaf
PHOTOS BY JOOYEON HA

Wendy Maruyama
The Watchtower | 2008
38 X 15 X 8 INCHES (96.5 X 38.1 X 20.3 CM)
Fir, pine, glass, image transfer
PHOTO BY NICK WU

Michael Cullen

One Thousand Suns | 2008

44 X 78 X 21 INCHES (111.8 X 198.1 X 53.3 CM)

Mahogany, milk paint, wenge, maple, Port Orford cedar

PHOTOS BY DON RUSSEL

Arnt Arntzen

Orca Table | 2008

66 X 36 X 17 INCHES (167.6 X 91.4 X 43.2 CM)

Elm, aluminum, aluminum airplane
propeller, varathane, lacquer

PHOTOS BY ARTIST

Michael Gloor

Bow-Front Entertainment Center | 2005

65 X 23 X 97 INCHES (165.1 X 58.4 X 246.4 CM)

Bubinga, chen chen veneer, bloodwood, black epoxy

PHOTO BY DAVID GILSTEIN

Steven M. White
Yin, Yang, and Young | 2006
48 X 36 X 15 INCHES (121.9 X 91.4 X 38.1 CM)
Cherry, spalted maple
PHOTO BY ARTIST

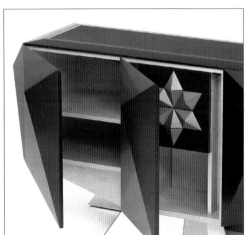

John Wiggers

Digitaria/Blue Star | 2009

34⅝ X 72 X 22 INCHES (87.9 X 182.9 X 55.9 CM)

Polyurethane, plywood, maple, stainless steel, black painted glass, solid maple dovetailed drawers, narra and padauk inlays

PHOTOS BY LORNE CHAPMAN

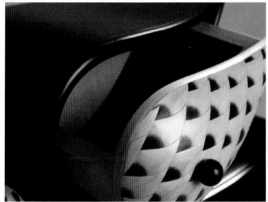

Kevin Irvin
Century Cabinet | 2006
72 X 16 X 16 INCHES (182.9 X 40.6 X 40.6 CM)
Smokey laurel burl, dyed maple
PHOTOS BY SCOTT BAXTER

Richard Judd

Dresser | 2007

54 X 38 X 22 INCHES (137.2 X 96.5 X 55.9 CM)

Birch plywood, bird's-eye maple,
lacewood, wenge, varnish finish

PHOTO BY BILL LEMKE

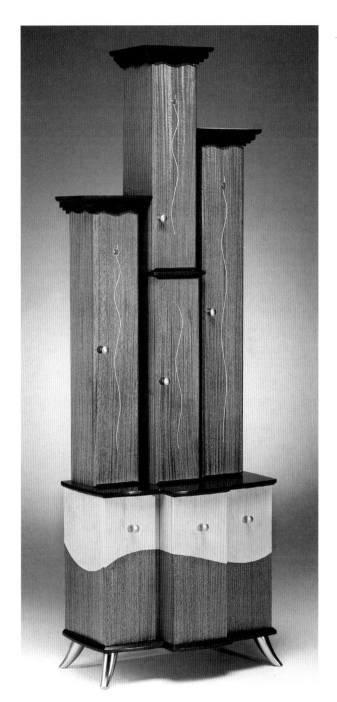

Michael Singer

Spano DVD Cabinet | 2006

80 X 25 X 16 INCHES (203.2 X 63.5 X 40.6 CM)

Mahogany, maple, wenge, aluminum, copper, abalone, varnish

Alexandra Snook
Edward Way
Hive Cabinet | 2009
65 X 26 X 9¼ INCHES (165.1 X 66 X 24.8 CM)
Bamboo, tinted lacquer
PHOTO BY ARTIST

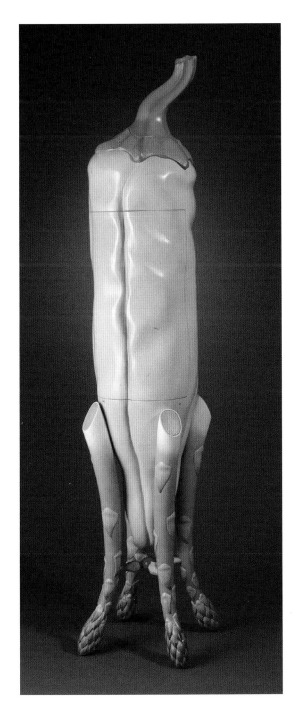

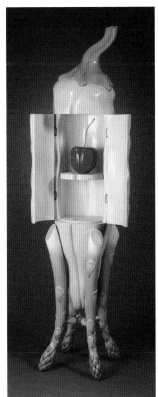

Craig Nutt

Banana Pepper Cabinet with Seeds and Fruit | 2001

81 X 17 X 17 INCHES (205.7 X 43.2 X 43.2 CM)

Acrylic lacquer, oil paint, wood

PHOTOS BY JOHN LUCAS

Mark Del Guidice

Leap and the Net Will Appear | 2008

25 X 22 X 7 INCHES (63.5 X 55.9 X 17.8 CM)

Curly maple, mahogany, medium
density fiberboard, milk paint, lacquer

PHOTOS BY CLEMENTS/HOWCROFT

Mordechai Schleifer
Bearer of 7 Boxes | 2000
71 X 20 X 21 INCHES (180.3 X 50.8 X 53.3 CM)
Cherry, aluminum
PHOTO BY JONATHAN RACHLINE

David Gates

Volume CD Cabinet | 2008

42³/₄ X 26¹/₄ X 15¹/₄ INCHES
(108.6 X 66.7 X 38.7 CM)

European oak, European brown oak,
American ash, cedar of Lebanon, steel,
vitreous enamel on steel

HANDLES BY HELEN CARNAC
PHOTO BY ARTIST

Steve Holman

Curly Oak Cabinet | 2004

79 X 41 X 20 INCHES (200.7 X 104.1 X 50.8 CM)

Curly red oak, purpleheart, padauk, lacquer

PHOTOS BY JOHN CONTE

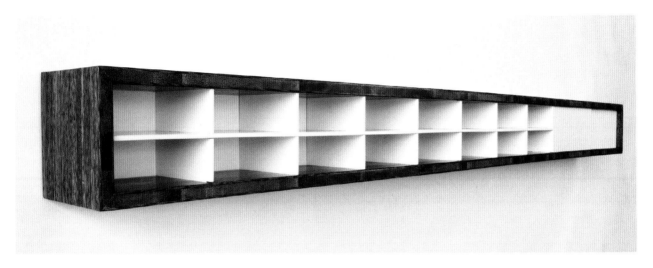

Jonny Doan
Untitled | 2008
6 X 70½ X 6 INCHES (15.2 X 179.1 X 15.2 CM)
Coconut palm, medium density fiberboard
PHOTO BY ARTIST

John Eric Byers
5 Ovals Dresser | 2004
56 X 41 X 24 INCHES (142.2 X 104.1 X 61 CM)
Mahogany, milk paint, iron, varnish, wax
PHOTO BY BILL BACHHUBER

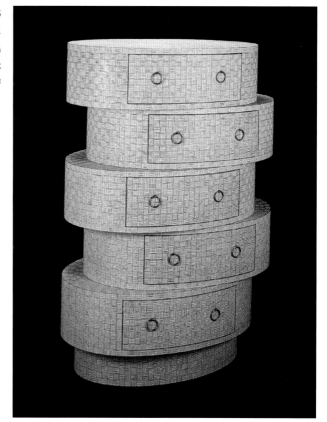

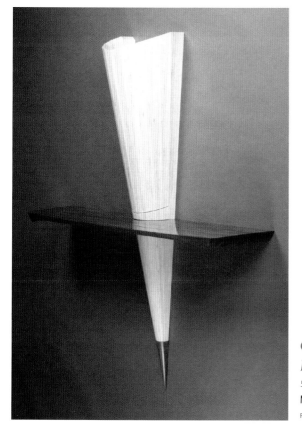

Cale Caboth
Faceted | 2008
56 X 48 X 12 INCHES (142.2 X 121.9 X 30.5 CM)
Maple, mahogany
PHOTO BY JIM DUGAN

Chris Martin

U Fleku (Jewelry Stand) | 2006

73 X 31 X 17 INCHES (185.4 X 78.7 X 43.2 CM)

Fabricated steel, bronze, Karelian birch, suede, Chechen, mirror glass

PHOTOS BY GEORGE ENSLEY

Christopher Atwood
Entertainment Console | 2008
21 X 47 X 12 INCHES (53.3 X 119.4 X 30.5 CM)
Maple, brass, shellac
PHOTO BY ARTIST

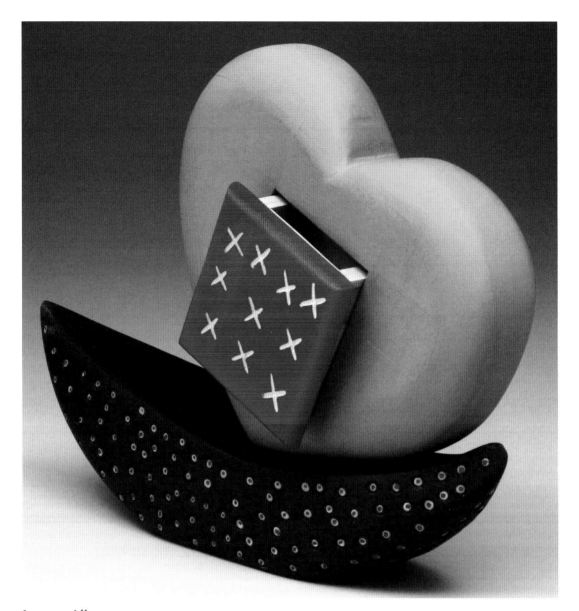

Jacque Allen
Heart Boat | 2007
10½ X 14 X 3¾ INCHES (26.7 X 35.6 X 9.5 CM)
Basswood
PHOTO BY ARTIST

Steven Samson

The Goal | 2005

38 X 21 X 15 INCHES (96.5 X 53.3 X 38.1 CM)

Mahogany, milk paint, vinyl, wax, found object

PHOTOS BY JEFFREY MEEUWSEN

Loyd Parker

Credenza | 2005

32 X 77 X 18 INCHES (81.3 X 195.6 X 45.7 CM)

Medium density fiberboard, powder-coated
screen, stainless steel

PHOTO BY RANDALL BOHL

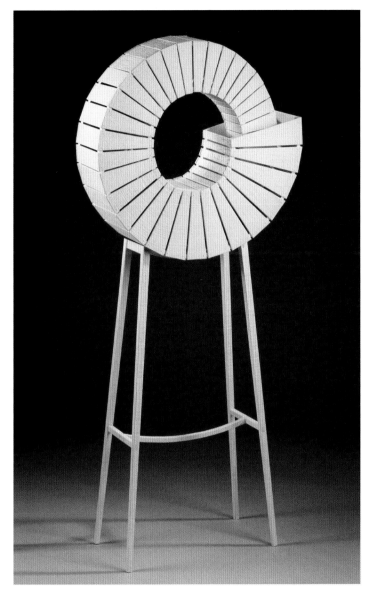

Don Miller

Uroboros | 2005

54 X 20 X 8 INCHES (137.2 X 50.8 X 20.3 CM)

White oak, wax

PHOTO BY MARK JOHNSON

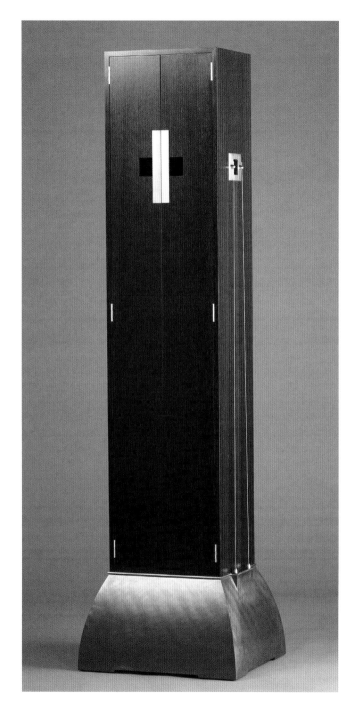

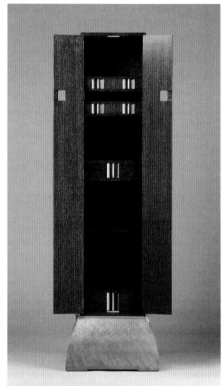

Richard Prisco
Chinese Cabinet | 2006
68 X 22 X 19 INCHES (172.7 X 55.9 X 48.3 CM)
Wenge, bamboo, nickel-plated steel, graphite
PHOTOS BY JOSEPH BYRD

Dave Boykin

Kimono Buffet | 2006

32 X 49 X 18 INCHES (81.3 X 124.5 X 45.7 CM)

Mahogany, pomele sapele, wenge

PHOTOS BY JIM STAYTON

James Schriber

Two-Door Cabinet #1 | 2006

75 X 30 X 16 INCHES (190.5 X 76.2 X 40.6 CM)

Milk paint, poplar, cherry, satin acrylic

PHOTO BY JOHN KANE

John Gallagher
Collector's Cabinet | 2008
51 X 25 X 13 INCHES (129.5 X 63.5 X 33 CM)
Silverash, Thuya burl, glass, lacquer finish
PHOTO BY PETRI KURKAA

Erinco König

Bowed-Front Media Console | 2006

27³/₄ X 67 X 20¹/₂ INCHES (70.4 X 170.2 X 52 CM)

Curly French walnut, black walnut, red alder, lacquer

PHOTO BY GORAN BASARIC

John Glendinning

Whiskey | 2004

33 X 16 X 16 INCHES (83.8 X 40.6 X 40.6 CM)

Mahogany, limestone, glass, brass, oil finish

PHOTOS BY ARTIST

Christoph Neander

Hanging Jewelry Cabinet | 2007

40 X 21 X 12 INCHES (101.6 X 53.3 X 30.5 CM)

Curly maple, claro walnut, Swiss pear, pomele sapele, dye, tung oil varnish

PHOTO BY ARTIST

Brian David Reid
Tartan Console | 2007
24 X 72 X 18 INCHES (61 X 182.9 X 45.7 CM)
Macassar ebony, padauk veneer, milk paint, oil varnish
PHOTO BY PATRICK MILLER

Petteri Leppikallio
Pörrö Sahlberg
Trilobite Cabin | 2009
13 X 11½ X 3 INCHES (33 X 29.2 X 7.6 CM)
Larch, dye, sand, polymer clay
PHOTOS BY ARTISTS

Pia Wüstenberg
Multistorage | 2008
55 X 47 X 25 INCHES (139.7 X 119.4 X 63.5 CM)
Birch plywood, clay, glaze, leather, lacquer
PHOTO BY PAUL JACQUES

Jenna Goldberg
Water and Leaves | 2009
75 X 28 X 16 INCHES (190.5 X 71.1 X 40.6 CM)
Basswood

PHOTOS BY MARK JOHNSON

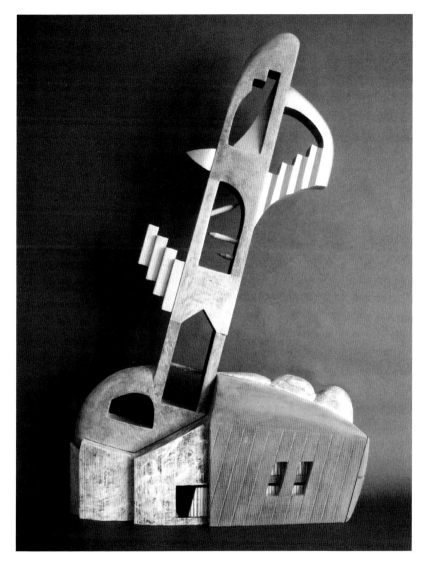

Arcisan (Bill) Garbus
ArchiTower | 2001
30 X 19 X 3 INCHES (76.2 X 48.3 X 7.6 CM)
Mahogany, poplar, pencils, twig,
gold and silver leaf, paint, shellac
PHOTOS BY ARTIST

Theodore Slavin
Peg-Leg CD Cabinet | 2007
54 X 15 X 15 INCHES (137.2 X 38.1 X 38.1 CM)
African bubinga, steel, brass, paint
PHOTO BY KIRK VAN ZANDBERGEN

Danny Kamerath
Carol | 2008
67 X 21 X 12½ INCHES (170.2 X 53.3 X 31.8 CM)
Leopard wood, cocobolo
PHOTO BY JOSEPH SAVANT

Jeffrey Meeuwsen
Classified | 2004
52 X 12 X 18½ INCHES (132.1 X 30.5 X 47 CM)
Mahogany, milk paint, acrylic paint,
watercolor pencil, wax
PHOTOS BY CHUCK HEINEY

Christopher Green
Taki Tansu (Waterfall Chest of Drawers) | 2009

23 X 10½ X 8 INCHES (58.4 X 26.7 X 20.3 CM)

Oak, Baltic plywood, poplar birch, rattan reed,
Chiyogami paper, acrylic paint, polyurethane finish

PHOTOS BY ARTIST

Anne Bossert

Nancy's Cabinet | 2007

14 X 17¼ X 13½ INCHES (35.6 X 43.8 X 34.3 CM)

Dyed Baltic birch plywood, dyed hand-woven
cotton, hinges, poly-acrylic finish

PHOTOS BY JOE MENDOZA

Pia Wüstenberg

Herber | 2007

12 X 12 X 8 INCHES (30.5 X 30.5 X 20.3 CM)

Cedar, clay, glaze, cork bark, wax

PHOTO BY ARTIST

Arthur Cadman
Rachel Cadman
Serpentine | 2008
35½ X 53 X 21 INCHES (90.2 X 134.6 X 53.3 CM)
Cherry, ripple sycamore
PHOTO BY ARTISTS

Doug Ives

Dragonfly | 2009

55 X 14 X 14 INCHES (139.7 X 35.6 X 35.6 CM)

Aframosia, zebrano, Port Orford
cedar, cocobolo, wenge, basswood

PHOTOS BY RAQUEL FORS

Shaun Fleming

Curly Koa Wall Cabinet | 2006

18 X 16 X 9½ INCHES (45.7 X 40.6 X 24.1 CM)

Koa, plywood, glass shelf, lacquer

PHOTO BY ROB RATKOWSKI

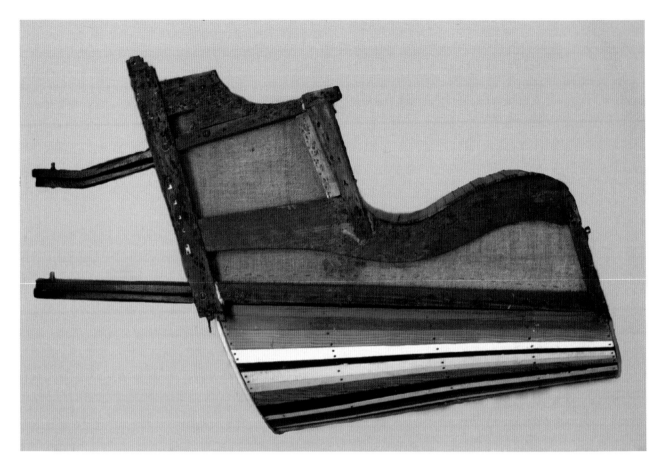

Stephen Whittlesey

Last Dance | 2007

30 X 44 X 11 INCHES (76.2 X 111.8 X 27.9 CM)

Salvaged chair parts, painted
strips, pine, mahogany, oil paint

PHOTOS BY RAOUL

Bart Niswonger

Striped Dresser | 2008

36 X 61 X 19 INCHES (91.4 X 154.9 X 48.3 CM)

Ash, paint, gloss finish

PHOTO BY ARTIST

Chris Martin
Autumn | 2007
42 X 55 X 27 INCHES (106.7 X 139.7 X 68.6 CM)
Painted wood, steel, leather, madrone,
afzelia burl, cast fine silver
PHOTOS BY GEORGE ENSLEY

Marcus Papay

Duality | 2009

30 X 8 X 16 INCHES (76.2 X 20.3 X 40.6 CM)

Steel, maple

PHOTOS BY AARON DRESSIN

Denise Bledsoe
Elfin Curio | 2006
19 X 18 X 10 INCHES (48.3 X 45.7 X 25.4 CM)
Oak, glass, mirror, oil satin, oil varnish
PHOTOS BY ARTIST

Anton Gerner
Burl Cabinet | 2005
52 X 60 X 24 INCHES (132.1 X 152.4 X 61 CM)
Burr elm, ebony inlays, aged bronze handles
PHOTO BY STEVEN PAM

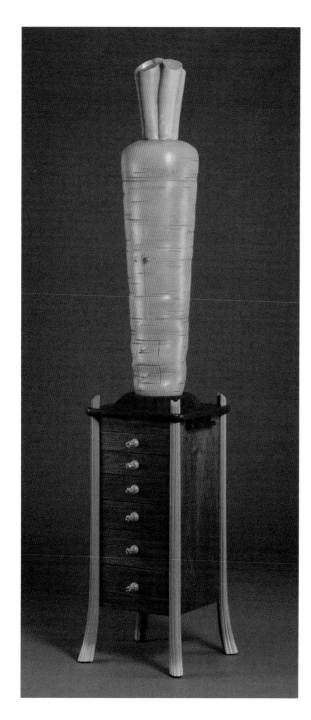

Craig Nutt
Nine-Carrot Treasure Chest | 2001
94 X 20 X 20 INCHES (238.8 X 50.8 X 50.8 CM)
Walnut, oil paint, maple, brass, glass
PHOTOS BY JOHN LUCAS

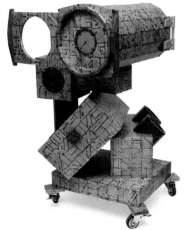

Fred Baier

Sensory Separator | 2005

49¹/₈ X 31⁷/₁₆ X 29¹/₂ INCHES (124.8 X 79.9 X 74.9 CM)

Solid maple, maple veneer, hardware, stain, lacquer

PHOTOS BY LUCY STRACHAM

Mats Fogelvik

The Jewel | 2009

32 X 60 X 16 INCHES (81.3 X 152.4 X 40.6 CM)

Koa, wenge, holly, pheasant wood,
mahogany, plywood, brass, glass, lacquer

PHOTO BY ARTIST

Thomas Nordstrom

Contemporary Chest | 2008

21 X 37 X 18 INCHES (53.3 X 94 X 45.7 CM)

Sapele, wenge, Japanese iron, polyurethane, wax

PHOTOS BY ED KESSLER

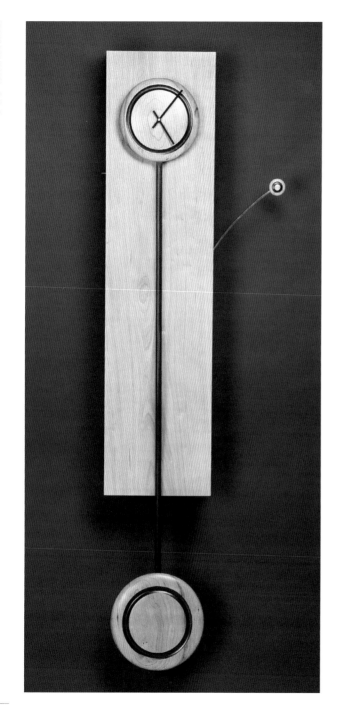

Jeff Johnson
Nifty Clock Cabinet | 2009
42 X 10 X 5 INCHES (106.7 X 25.4 X 12.7 CM)
Cherry, stainless steel
PHOTOS BY AL NOWAK

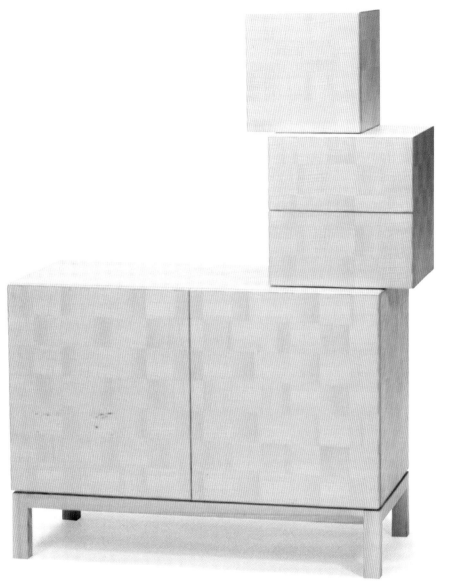

Jong Hyuk Jang
Checker Pattern | 2008
18 X 36 X 18 INCHES (45.7 X 91.4 X 45.7 CM)
Ash veneer, ash, clear satin lacquer
PHOTO BY ARTIST

Joseph Walsh
Collector's Cabinet | 2006
64 X 50 X 26 INCHES (162.6 X 127 X 66 CM)
Olive ash, oak, bronze
PHOTOS BY ANDREW BRADLEY

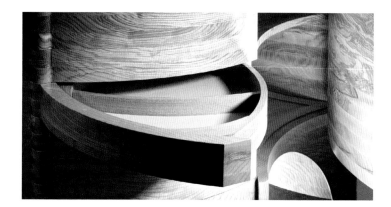

Aaron Fedarko

Teak Cabinet | 2008

21¼ X 37 X 26 INCHES (54 X 94 X 66 CM)

Teak, oil

PHOTO BY JIM DUGAN

Gregg Lipton

Three-Squared Cabinet | 2002

68 X 48 X 22 INCHES (172.7 X 121.9 X 55.9 CM)

Tineo, ebonized maple, satin lacquer

PHOTO BY DENNIS GRIGGS

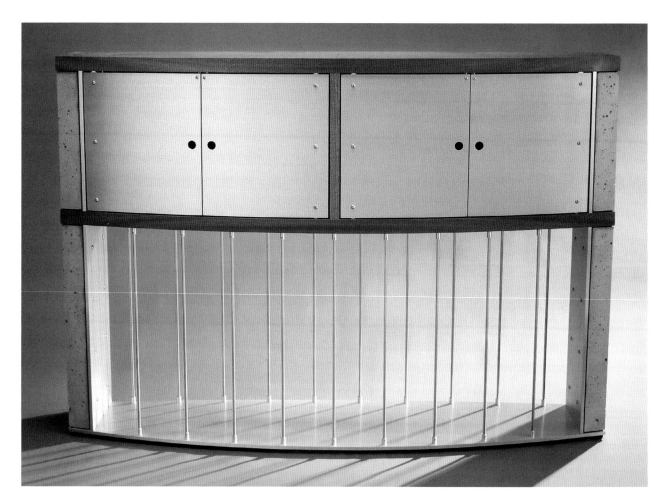

Peter Harrison

Liquor Cabinet | 2009

42 X 60 X 12 INCHES (106.7 X 152.4 X 30.5 CM)

Mahogany, aluminum, stainless steel, concrete, lacquer

PHOTOS BY STOCKSTUDIOSPHOTOGRAPHY.COM

Brent Skidmore
Pale Ostrich-Skin Side Table | 2008
31 X 31 X 16 INCHES (78.7 X 78.7 X 40.6 CM)
Maple, basswood, glass, paint
PHOTO BY DAVID RAMSEY

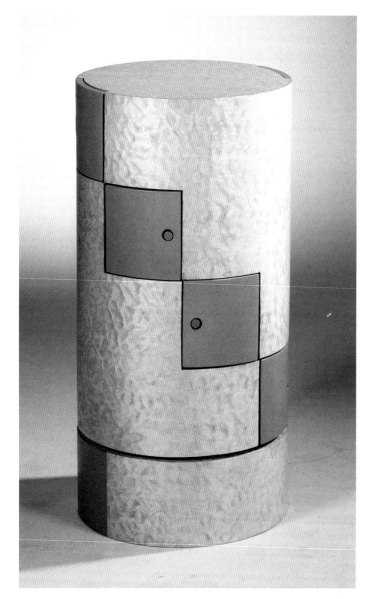

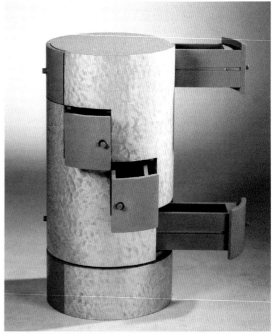

Srdjan Simić
Drawered Swivel | 2001
30 X 15 X 15 INCHES (76.2 X 38.1 X 38.1 CM)
Plywood, pearl veneer, milk paint
PHOTOS BY ARTIST

Jack Rodie

Za Zen | 2006

32 X 12 X 12 INCHES (81.3 X 30.5 X 30.5 CM)

Bird's-eye maple, cherry

PHOTO BY ARTIST

Nicole Runde

Strata | 2008

28 X 7 X 6½ INCHES (71.1 X 17.8 X 16.5 CM)

Laser-cut corrugated cardboard, maple-veneered
plywood, aluminum, paint, lacquer

PHOTO BY WAYNE MOORE

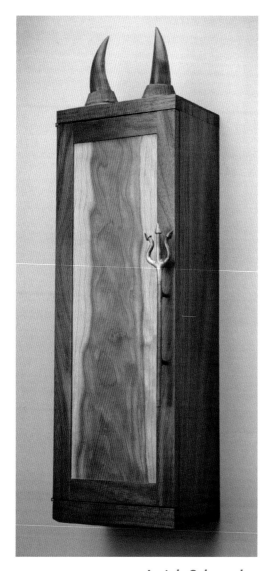

Isaiah Schroeder

Whiskey, You're the Devil | 2007

30 X 10 X 7 INCHES (76.2 X 25.4 X 17.8 CM)

Walnut, cherry, bronze, oil paint

PHOTOS BY WILLIAM LEMKE

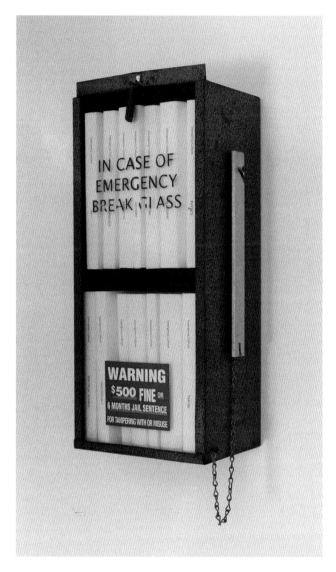

Christy Oates

Emergency Culture | 2008

19 X 9 X 6 INCHES (48.3 X 22.9 X 15.2 CM)

Steel, glass, books, paint

PHOTO BY ARTIST

J.M. Syron
Bonnie Bishoff
Iris Cabinet | 2008
62 X 24 X 18 INCHES (157.5 X 61 X 45.7 CM)
African mahogany, bubinga veneer, polymer clay veneer
PHOTOS BY DEAN POWELL

Christoph Neander

China Cabinet | 2007

99 X 60 X 20 INCHES (251.5 X 152.4 X 50.8 CM)

Honduran mahogany, hand-blown art glass, brass hinges, tung oil varnish

HAND-BLOWN GLASS BY JULIE CONWAY
PHOTOS BY JOE PICARD

Garry Knox Bennett

Nail Cabinet | 1979

74 X 24 X 17 INCHES (187.9 X 60.9 X 43.2 CM)

Padauk, glass, lamp parts,
copper, nail, steel wire

PHOTOS BY M. LEE FATHERREE

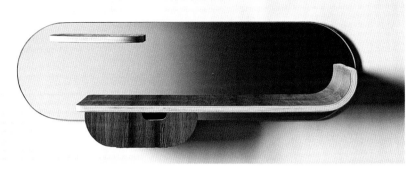

Heather Wenz

Oblong | 2009

28 X 8 X 7 INCHES (71.1 X 20.3 X 17.8 CM)

Italian bending ply, teak veneer, white laminate, glass mirror

PHOTO BY WAYNE MOORE

Erin Dace Behling

Dressing Table | 2008

61½ X 30 X 14½ INCHES
(156.2 X 76.2 X 35.6 CM)

Plywood, veneer, paint, stain, mirror glass

PHOTO BY ARTIST

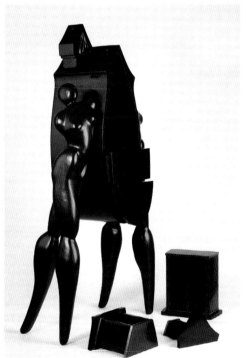

Rebecca Goodman
The Sisters | 2005
32 X 18 X 12 INCHES (81.2 X 45.7 X 30.5 CM)
Poplar, paint, gold leaf
PHOTOS BY LARRY STANLEY

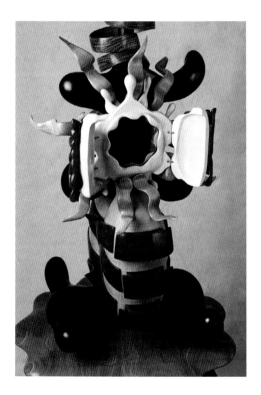

Lepo
Untitled | 2004
74 X 28 X 28 INCHES (188 X 71.1 X 71.1 CM)
Wenge, cherry, zebrawood, pickled
maple, makore, purpleheart, cocobolo
PHOTOS BY MICHAEL AYERS

Isaac Arms

End Table Crank Box | 2003

27 X 14 X 14 INCHES (68.6 X 35.6 X 35.6 CM)

Mahogany, steel, maple, Douglas fir, milk paint

PHOTOS BY BILL LEMKE

Burnell Yow!

Balance | 1998

28 X 12 X 6 INCHES (71.1 X 30.5 X 15.2 CM)

Wood, crystal

PHOTO BY ARTIST

Trevor Hadden

Grandma Marie's Celtic Cabinet | 2008

23 X 13 X 7 INCHES (58.4 X 33 X 17.8 CM)

Cherry, soft maple, pheasant
wood, milk paint, tung oil, shellac

PHOTOS BY DON RUSSEL

Gregg Lipton

Gazelle Sideboard | 1992

31 X 60 X 20 INCHES (78.7 X 152.4 X 50.8 CM)

Bird's-eye maple, mahogany, rosewood, oil varnish

PHOTO BY DENNIS GRIGGS

Zach Malcolm
Untitled | 2009
65½ X 20 X 15¾ INCHES (166.4 X 50.8 X 40 CM)
White oak, ash, ebony
PHOTOS BY GARY ROGOWSKI

Jordan Goodman

Watch Winder | 2009

18 X 18 X 12 INCHES (45.7 X 45.7 X 30.5 CM)

Honduran mahogany, tiger maple, black
leather, aluminum, glass, conversion varnish

PHOTO BY JIM DUGAN

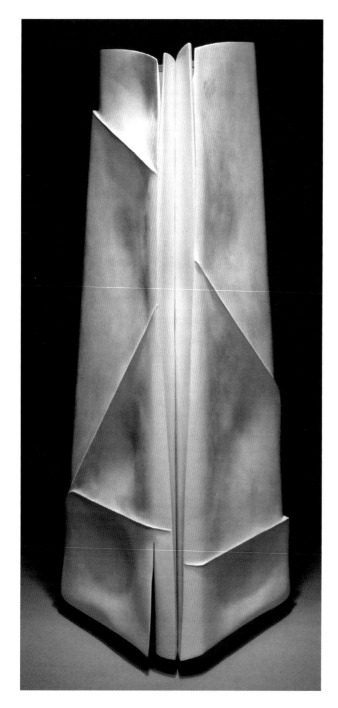

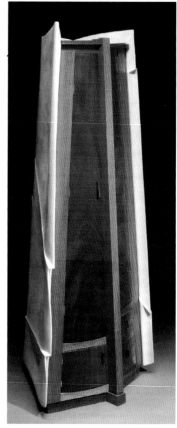

Gian-Paul Piane
Untitled | 2003
36 X 30 X 67 INCHES (91.4 X 76.2 X 170.2 CM)
Mahogany, poplar, milk paint, gel varnish
PHOTOS BY GEOFF TESCH

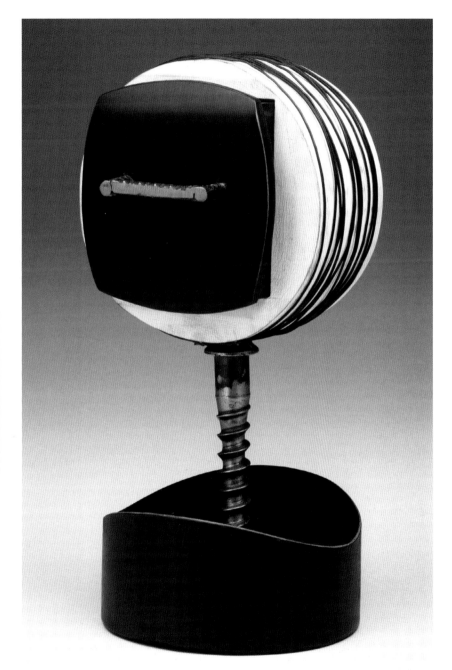

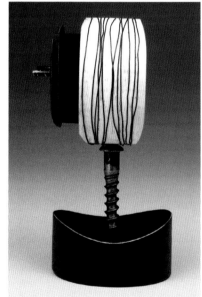

Jacque Allen
Heavy Metal | 2006
18 X 8 X 6 INCHES (45.7 X 20.3 X 15.2 CM)
Rebar, tie wire, railroad spike, basswood
PHOTOS BY ARTIST

Phillip Mann
Shrine Jewelry Box | 2004
15 X 19 X 11 INCHES (38.1 X 48.3 X 27.9 CM)
Lacewood veneers, mahogany
PHOTOS BY CHARLIE ROY

Yoav S. Liberman
Six Pack | 2005
10 X 5½ X 18 INCHES (25.4 X 14 X 45.7 CM)
Reclaimed heart pine, wenge, aluminum, brass
PHOTOS BY DEAN POWELL

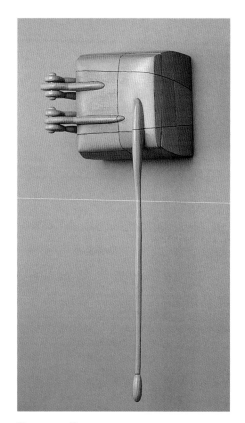

Reagan Furqueron

Checker 2 | 2002

12 X 5 X 5 INCHES (30.5 X 12.7 X 12.7 CM)

Mahogany, milk paint

PHOTO BY ARTIST

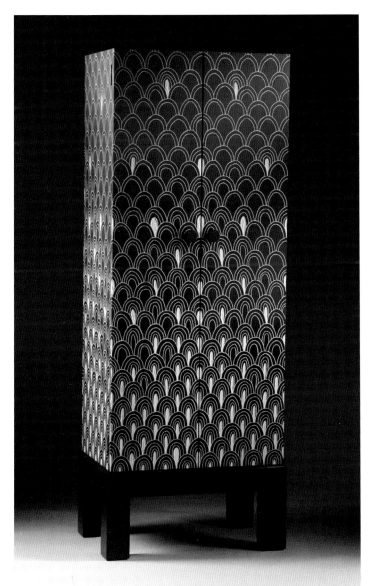

Jenna Goldberg
Blue Bijou | 2008
75 X 28 X 17 INCHES (190.5 X 71.1 X 43.2 CM)
Basswood

PHOTOS BY MARK JOHNSON

Michael Hoffer

Homage to Suzuki Roshi | 2006

27 X 12½ X 5½ INCHES (68.6 X 31.8 X 14 CM)

White oak, bone, stone disks, waxed linen thread, paper

PHOTOS BY DANIEL BARSOTTI

Charlotte Kubiak
Key Cabinet | 2009
16 X 9 X 2½ INCHES (40.6 X 22.9 X 6.4 CM)
Marine plywood, Masonite,
Philippine mahogany, koa
PHOTO BY ARTIST

Matthew Thomas Malesky

Plateau | 2008

4½ X 7 X 12 INCHES (11.4 X 17.8 X 30.5 CM)

Cherry, maple, walnut, milk paint, oil

PHOTO BY ARTIST

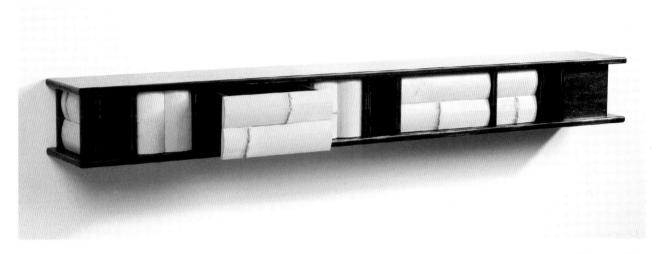

Carter Sio

Shelf with Drawers, Wall Hung | 2007

6 X 45 X 8 INCHES (15.2 X 114.3 X 20.3 CM)

Ebonized Baltic birch, bamboo

PHOTO BY JIM DUGAN

Gary Upton

Hawaii Wave Cabinet | 2006

92 X 84 X 24 INCHES (233.7 X 213.4 X 61 CM)

Western maple, ebony, laser-engraved
photo on aluminum, gold leaf, tung oil

PHOTO BY ARTIST

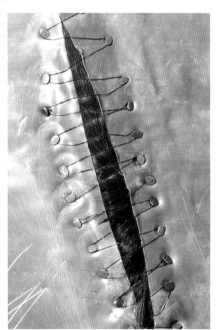

Wendy Maruyama
Vanity | 2006
55 X 16 X 16 INCHES (139.7 X 40.6 X 40.6 CM)
Pau ferro, silk, jade, video components
PHOTOS BY DEAN POWELL

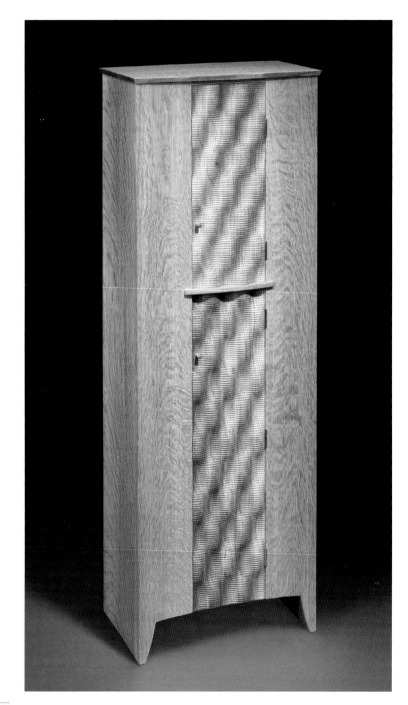

Rich Tannen

Cupboard | 2006

45 X 15 X 9 INCHES (114.3 X 38.1 X 22.9 CM)

White oak, wax

PHOTOS BY GEOFF TESCH

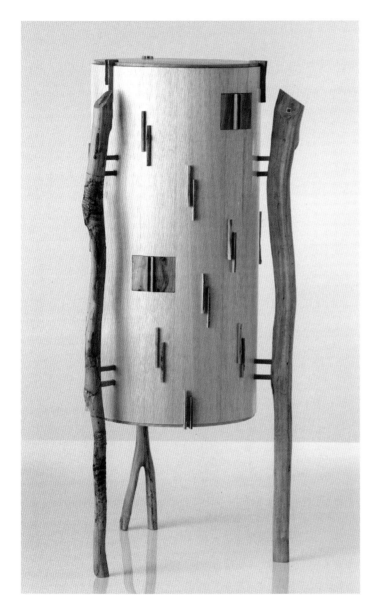

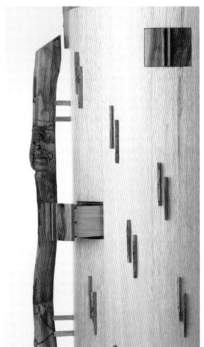

Wayne Petrie
In Transition Sculptural Cabinet | 2007
29 X 12 INCHES (73.7 X 30.5 CM)
Tasmanian oak, weeping ti tree
PHOTOS BY DAVID SANDISON

Reagan Furqueron

White-Wall Cabinet | 2006

72 X 9 X 4 INCHES (182.9 X 22.9 X 10.2 CM)

Mahogany, oak, milk paint

PHOTOS BY MARK JOHNSTON

Don Miller
Sidelong | 2005
50 X 14 X 14 INCHES (127 X 35.6 X 35.6 CM)
White oak, wax
PHOTO BY MARK JOHNSON

Ken Richards

Secretary | 2005

104 X 44 X 25 INCHES (264.2 X 111.8 X 63.5 CM)

Figured European pear, ebony, sterling silver, oil/wax finish

PHOTOS BY ROBERT MCCRORY

Blaise Gaston
Liquor Cabinet | 2000
84 X 40 X 25 INCHES (213.4 X 101.6 X 63.5 CM)
Bee's-wing andiroba, mahogany,
granite, glass, tung oil
PHOTOS BY PHILIP BEAURLINE

Damon McIntyre

People under the Stairs | 2008

60 X 36 X 6 INCHES (152.4 X 91.4 X 15.2 CM)

Red oak, walnut, yellowheart, neon light

PHOTO BY ARTIST

Matthew Werner
Showcase Cabinet | 2007
60 X 21 X 12 INCHES (152.4 X 53.3 X 30.5 CM)
Walnut, yaka, granadillo, brass, glass, shellac,
wax, yellowheart, mahogany and wenge inlays
PHOTO BY PAUL TITANGOS

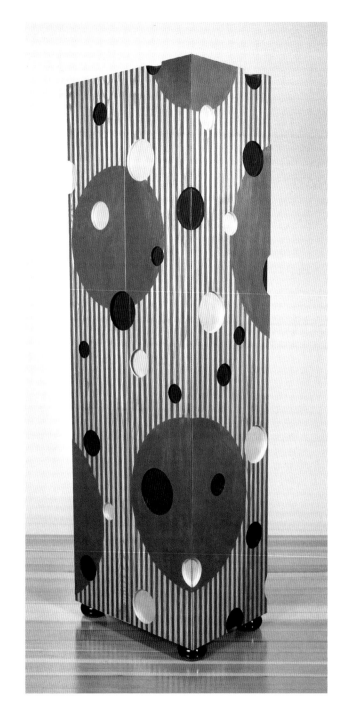

Bart Niswonger
Striped Armoire | 2008
72 X 24 X 16 INCHES (182.9 X 61 X 40.6 CM)
Ash, paint, gloss finish
PHOTOS BY ARTIST

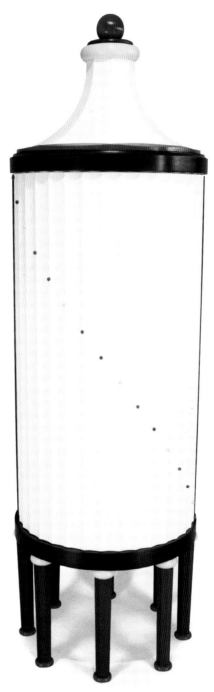

Ken Guenter
Polka | 2004
72 X 21 INCHES (182.8 X 53.3 CM)
Poplar, birch and mahogany
veneers, acrylic paint
PHOTO BY ARTIST

Loyd Parker

Entertainment Center/Display | 2007

57 X 151 X 19 INCHES (144.8 X 383.5 X 48.3 CM)

Maple, glass, stainless steel

PHOTO BY RANDALL BOHL

Jacob Knudsen
Negative Idea | 2004
35 X 61 X 25 INCHES (88.9 X 154.9 X 63.5 CM)
Maple, painted steel, oil varnish
PHOTO BY TYLER MARSHALL

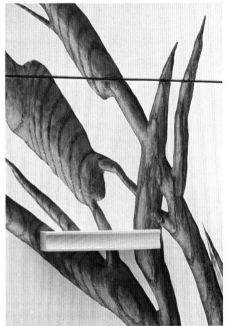

Duncan Gowdy
Dresser with Glacial Shadow | 2008
54 X 33 X 18 INCHES (137.2 X 83.8 X 45.7 CM)
Ash, quarter-sawn maple, satin
PHOTOS BY DEAN POWELL

Greg Moffatt
Tall Oval | 2007
52 X 16 X 13 INCHES (132.1 X 40.6 X 33 CM)
Spalted sycamore, maple, shellac
PHOTOS BY DAVID WALTER

Floyd Gompf
Yellow Tower | 2001

70 X 22 X 16 INCHES (177.8 X 55.9 X 40.6 CM)

Found wood, found hardware

PHOTO BY RICHARD HELLYER

Walter D. Welch
W. Douglas Allen
Big Red | 2004

84 X 54 X 18 INCHES (213.4 X 137.2 X 45.7 CM)

Formica, luan plywood, steel, stainless steel, rubber gasket

PHOTO BY GWEN AUCOIN

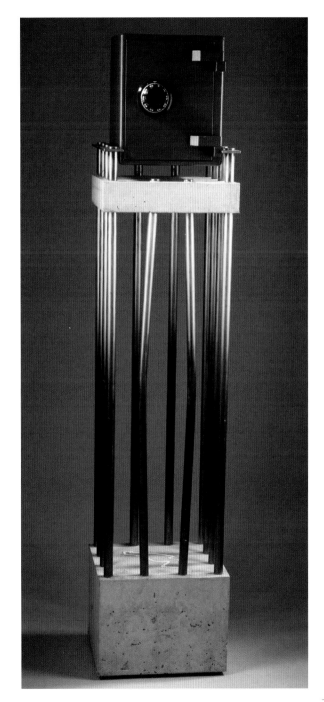

Joel Green
Public Enemy #1 | 2007
66½ X 14½ X 13 INCHES (168.9 X 36.8 X 33 CM)
Medium density fiberboard, mild steel, concrete,
ink, paint, composition leaf, found object
PHOTOS BY MARK JOHNSTON

Toby Winteringham

Untitled | 2009

36 X 54 X 16 INCHES (91.4 X 137.2 X 40.6 CM)

Bog oak, cedar of Lebanon, colored bolivar
marquetry, handmade brass hinges, glass top

PHOTO BY ARTIST

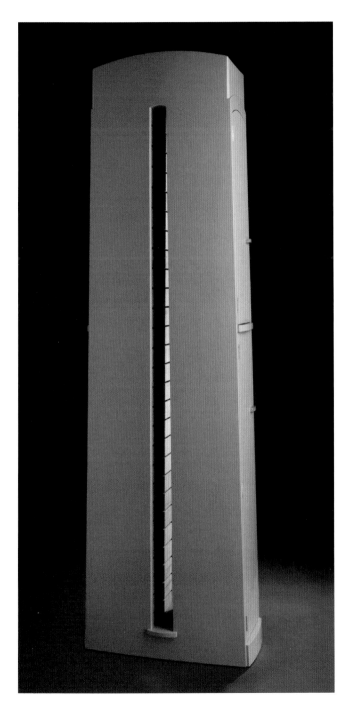

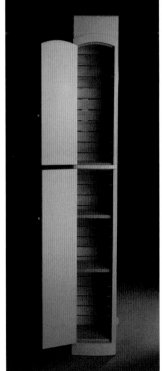

Will Tracey

Chimney Cupboard | 2008

82 X 25 X 14 INCHES (208.3 X 63.5 X 35.6 CM)

Mahogany, Douglas fir, paint, graphite

PHOTOS BY ELIZABETH LAMARK

Jacque Allen

Asheville's Steep Slope Housing | 2007

28 X 20 X 14 INCHES (71.1 X 50.8 X 35.6 CM)

Rebar, copper, tin, basswood

PHOTO BY ARTIST

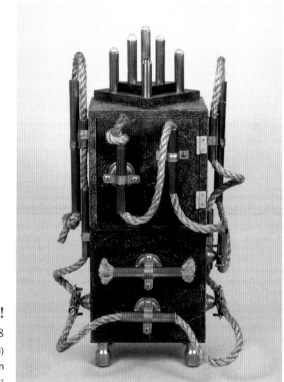

Burnell Yow!

Ceci N'est Pas une Boite a Tiroirs | 1998

24 X 12 X 5 INCHES (61 X 30.5 X 12.7 CM)

Wood, pipes, iron

PHOTO BY ARTIST

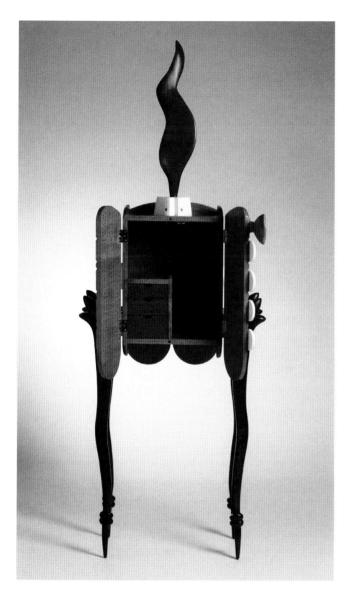

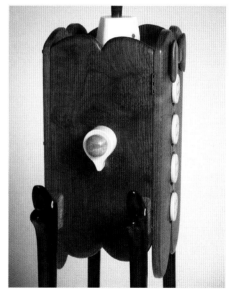

Dale Lewis

Fashionably Famous | 2007

88 X 32 X 14½ INCHES (223.5 X 81.3 X 36.8 CM)

Lacewood, cherry, birch, maple,
cocobolo, Corian, lacquer

PHOTOS BY RALPH ANDERSON

Naushon Hale

Burned Case No. 3 | 2007

10 X 12 X 16 INCHES (25.4 X 30.5 X 40.6 CM)

Scorched ash

PHOTOS BY ARTIST

Dan Allaire
Wine Table | 2002
76 X 36 X 18 INCHES (193 X 91.4 X 45.7 CM)
Alder wood, walnut finish, silver leaf
PHOTO BY KELLY CAPPELLI

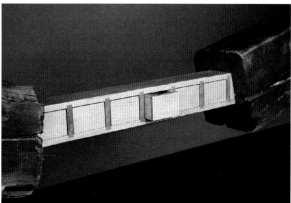

Thomas Shields

Same on the Inside | 2008

11 X 46 X 9 INCHES (27.9 X 116.8 X 22.9 CM)

Railroad tie, cherry

PHOTOS BY ARTIST

Shaun Bullens

K.I. Reliquary | 2007

30 X 4½ X 12 INCHES (76.2 X 11.4 X 30.5 CM)

Native Australian timber, kangaroo vertebrae

PHOTO BY ARTIST

David Goldenberg

Ovaltino Bed Table | 2004

30 X 30 X 20 INCHES (76.2 X 76.2 X 50.8 CM)

Walnut, pearl inlay

PHOTO BY RORY EARNSHAW

Ken Guenter
Minuet | 2004
70 X 21 INCHES (177.8 X 53.3 CM)
Honduran mahogany, wenge, makare,
birch and mahogany veneers, oil finish
PHOTO BY ARTIST

Kate Davidson

Cecilia | 2009

50⅛ X 12 X 15⅝ INCHES (127.3 X 30.5 X 39.7 CM)

Jatoba, maple, plywood, veneer, staples, foam, muslin, satin, thread, screws, hinges, knobs

PHOTOS BY ARTIST

Fred Baier
Time Capsule | 2006
78⁹/₁₆ X 78⁹/₁₆ X 98¹/₄ INCHES (199.5 X 199.5 X 249.6 CM)
Sycamore, glass, stainless steel, stain, lacquer
PHOTOS BY ARTIST

Melia (Partners: John-Paul Melia and Lucy Tatam)

I Drawers | 1999

23 X 65 X 13 INCHES (60 X 166 X 33 CM)

Medium density fiberboard, polyurethane lacquer

PHOTO BY 2020 PV

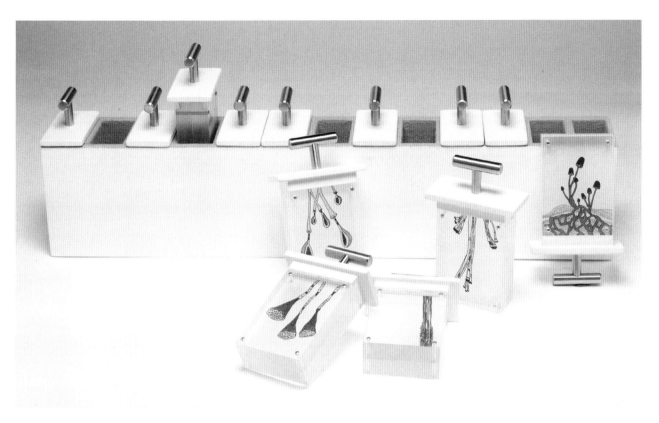

Kelly Rudman

Specimen Archive | 2008

6 X 4½ X 26 INCHES (15.2 X 11.4 X 66 CM)

Maple, clear plastic sheeting, felt, metal, paper, ink

PHOTOS BY JAY YORK

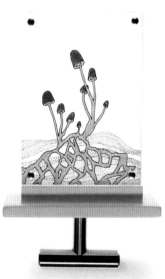

Megan Christie

Renew Art Cabinet | 2008

53 X 28 X 12½ INCHES (134.6 X 71.1 X 31.8 CM)

Western Australian blackbutt, Tasmanian myrtle veneer, tiger myrtle, musk, walnut, red cedar, New Guinea rosewood, eucalyptus veneers, orange oil

PHOTO BY NEIL ERASMUS

Dave Boykin
Cloud Buffet | 2008
33 X 73 X 21 INCHES (83.8 X 185.4 X 53.3 CM)
Cherry, ebony pulls
PHOTO BY RON RUSCIO

Duncan Gowdy

Sideboard | 2006

33 X 54 X 18 INCHES (83.8 X 137.2 X 45.7 CM)

Ash, quartersawn white oak, stain

PHOTO BY DEAN POWELL

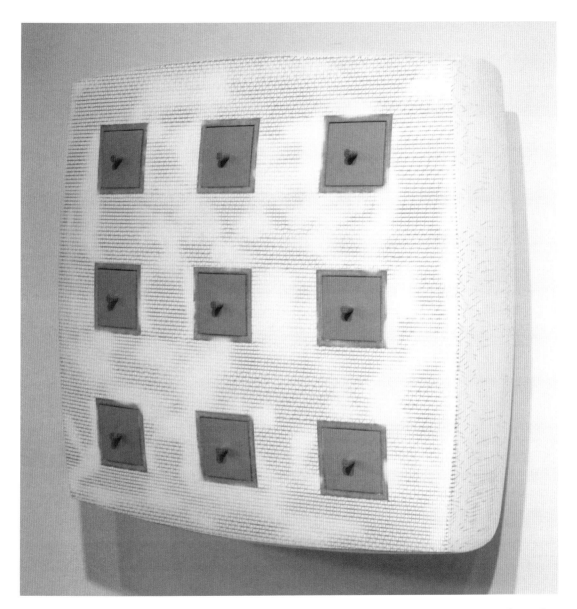

Jason Schneider
Tic-Tac-Toe | 2008
20 X 20 X 9 INCHES (50.8 X 50.8 X 22.9 CM)
Corrugated cardboard, plaster, ash, milk paint
PHOTO BY ARTIST

Jim Oleson

Mesquite Buffet | 2004

36¹⁄₂ X 65³⁄₄ X 19³⁄₄ INCHES (92.7 X 167 X 50.2 CM)

Mesquite, maple, wenge, oil varnish, milk paint

PHOTO BY ARTIST

Arnold d'Epagnier

Wine Cabinet | 2005

76 X 48 X 24 INCHES (193 X 121.9 X 61 CM)

Cherry, ebony, glass, various marquetry
veneers, electric light, oil, wax, satin finish

PHOTOS BY MICHAEL LATIC

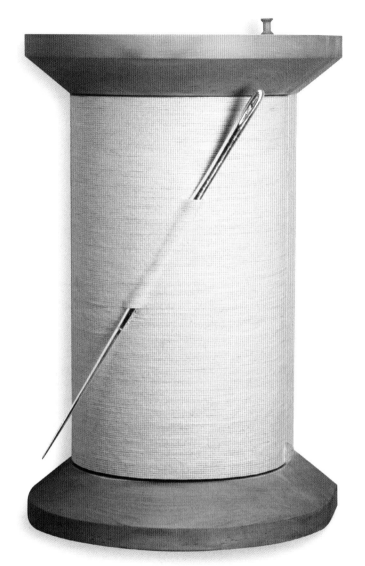

Peter Dellert
Thread Spool Cabinet | 2004
32 X 22 X 15 INCHES (81.3 X 55.9 X 38.1 CM)
Basswood, rope, silver-leaf mahogany, needle,
dyed bird's-eye maple, integral lighting, objects
PHOTOS BY JOHN POLAK

Alison J. McLennan
Metamorphosis Jewelry Cabinet #1 | 2008
22¼ X 16 X 9 INCHES (56.5 X 40.6 X 22.9 CM)
Yellow satinwood, fiberglass, mahogany,
brass, copper, laminate, lacquer
PHOTO BY ARTIST

Maurine Pasi

Tiny Cabinet | 2008

13½ X 9 X 4 INCHES (34.3 X 22.9 X 10.2 CM)

Madrone, Western maple, brass, glass, shellac

PHOTOS BY DAVID WELTER

John Lee
Carraig | 2006
34 X 63 X 24 INCHES (86.4 X 160 X 61 CM)
White oak, leather, acrylic flat matte lacquer
PHOTO BY TREVOR HARTE

Blaise Gaston

Lelia's Dresser | 1998

48 X 66 X 22 INCHES (121.9 X 167.6 X 55.9 CM)

Bubinga, curly maple, fishtail oak, tung oil

PHOTO BY ALAN HOUSEL

Jennifer Anderson

Ellipse | 2000

10 X 10¾ X 7¾ INCHES (25.4 X 27.3 X 19.7 CM)

Pear, machiche, maple

PHOTOS BY LARRY STANLEY

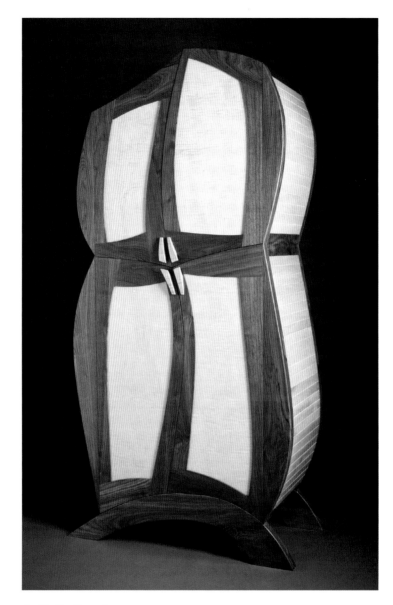

Seth Rolland

Hayes Entertainment Center | 2007

76 X 44 X 23 INCHES (193 X 111.8 X 58.4 CM)

Walnut, maple, curly maple

PHOTO BY FRANK ROSS

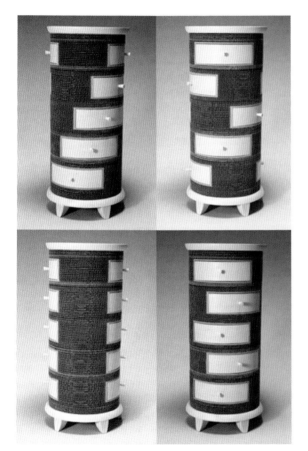

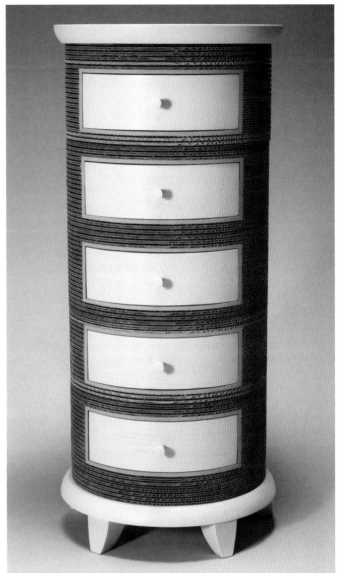

Jason Schneider

Spin | 2007

36 X 17 INCHES (91.4 X 43.2 CM)

Corrugated cardboard, ash, milk paint

PHOTOS BY ARTIST

Duncan Gowdy
Wall Cabinet with Branches | 2009
32 X 20 X 8 INCHES (81.3 X 50.8 X 20.3 CM)
Ash, rift-sawn white oak, stain
PHOTO BY DEAN POWELL

Jamie Womack
All Way Cabinet | 2004
68 X 12 X 12 INCHES (172.7 X 30.5 X 30.5 CM)
Sapele, maple plywood, birch, maple
PHOTOS BY ARTIST

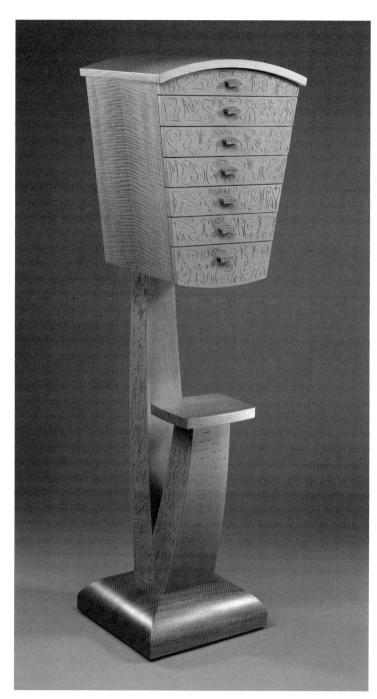

Mark Del Guidice

Adornmeant | 2007

57 X 18 X 16 INCHES (144.8 X 45.7 X 40.6 CM)

Figured makore, mahogany, basswood, cherry, fabric, milk paint, varnish

PHOTO BY CLEMENTS/HOWCROFT

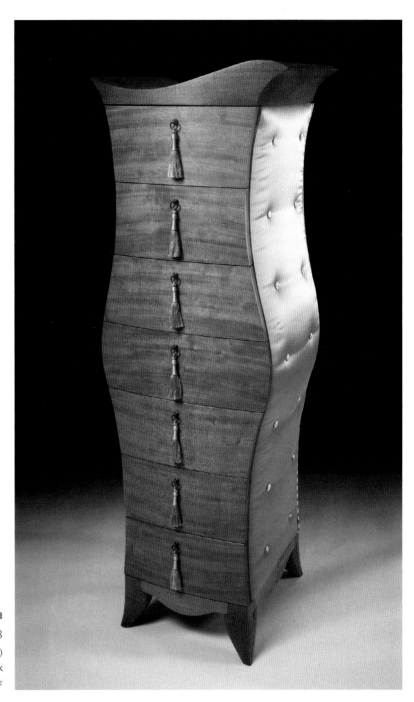

Katherine Ortega
Lingerie Chest of Drawers | 2008
65 X 23 X 21 INCHES (165.1 X 58.4 X 53.3 CM)
Mahogany, plywood, silk
PHOTO BY ARTIST

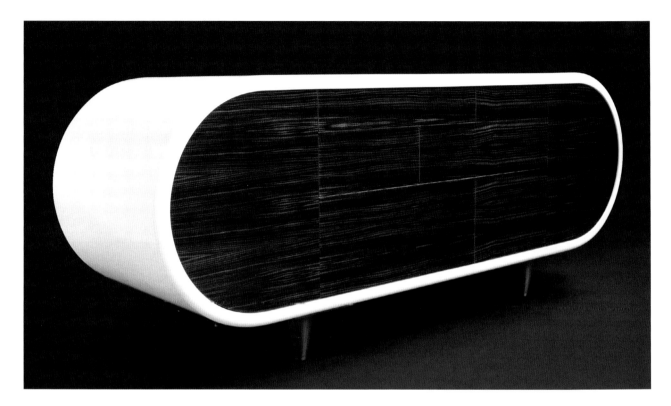

Gareth Brown

Orbit Credenza | 2006

30 X 24 X 78 INCHES (76.2 X 61 X 198.1 CM)

Macassar ebony, American black walnut, rock maple, stainless steel, medium density fiberboard, acrylic lacquer

PHOTOS BY KEITH LEIGHTON

Timothy Maddox

Naked Came the Weekend | 2007

56 X 28 X 18 INCHES (142.2 X 71.1 X 45.7 CM)

Steel, Douglas fir, patina, paint, lacquer

PHOTOS BY TIM BARNWELL

Katie Hudnall

Cabinet with Sidecar | 2008

24 X 24 X 16 INCHES (61 X 61 X 40.6 CM)

Plywood, medium density fiberboard, poplar, maple, glass, copper, paint, ink, lacquer

PHOTOS BY TAYLOR DABNEY

Vincent Leman

The Acrobats | 2007

64 X 26 X 16 INCHES (162.6 X 66 X 40.6 CM)

Birch plywood, acrylic paint, waterborne urethane

PHOTO BY ARTIST

Martin Lane

Bookcase | 1999

75 X 45¾ X 19½ INCHES (190.5 X 116.2 X 49.5 CM)

English cherry, burr walnut, satin matte lacquer, brass

PHOTO BY BLANTERN & DAVIS LIMITED

Kyle Fleet

Jewelry Box | 2009

25 X 15 X 11 INCHES (63.5 X 38.1 X 27.9 CM)

White oak, walnut, brass, oil varnish

PHOTOS BY BRIANA TRUDELL

Margaret Polcawich

Wine Cabinet | 2007

37 X 60 X 18 INCHES (94 X 152.4 X 45.7 CM)

Cherry, curly maple, walnut, polymer
clay, paint, pewter, oil, wax

PHOTO BY ARTIST

Nicola D'Agnone

Rocks on the Beach | 2009

30 X 36 X 11 INCHES (76.2 X 91.4 X 27.9 CM)

Beech, river rocks, steel, stain, lacquer, epoxy coating

Neal Barrett

Liquor Cabinet | 2007

54 X 36 X 21 INCHES (137.2 X 91.4 X 53.3 CM)

Mahogany, wenge, oil

PHOTO BY ARTIST

Brian Hubel
Ollie's World | 2006
25 X 53 X 20 INCHES (63.5 X 134.6 X 50.8 CM)
Cherry, ebonized ash, ebony
PHOTO BY DON JONES

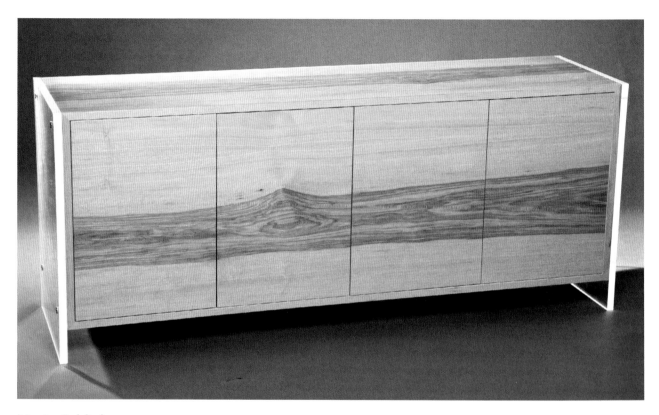

Mario Sabljak

Simplicity | 2008

24 X 56 X 17 INCHES (61 X 142.2 X 43.2 CM)

Hickory, acrylic, glass, lacquer

PHOTO BY WENDY D.

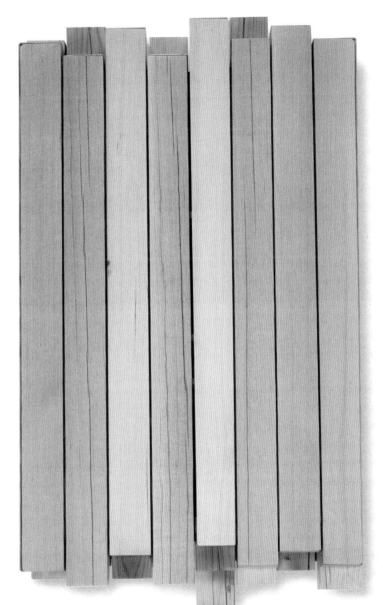

David Rasmussen

Bundle | 2009

36 X 22 X 10 INCHES (91.4 X 55.9 X 25.4 CM)

Reclaimed fur, cocobolo, tung oil/varnish, European hinge

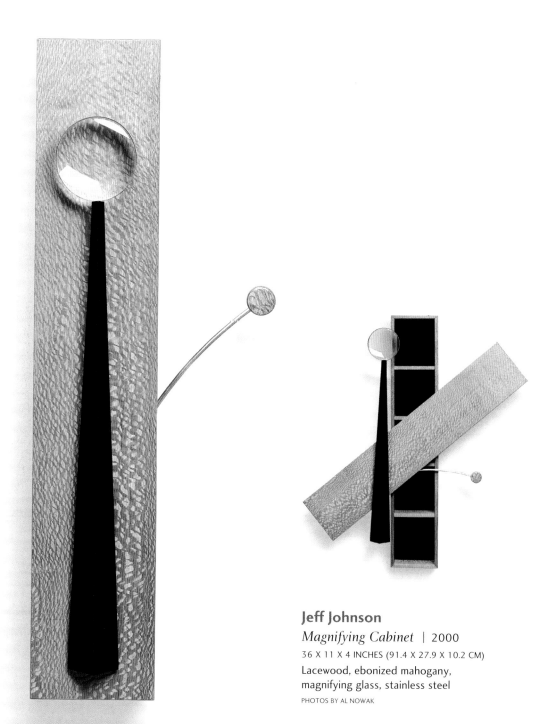

Jeff Johnson

Magnifying Cabinet | 2000

36 X 11 X 4 INCHES (91.4 X 27.9 X 10.2 CM)

Lacewood, ebonized mahogany, magnifying glass, stainless steel

PHOTOS BY AL NOWAK

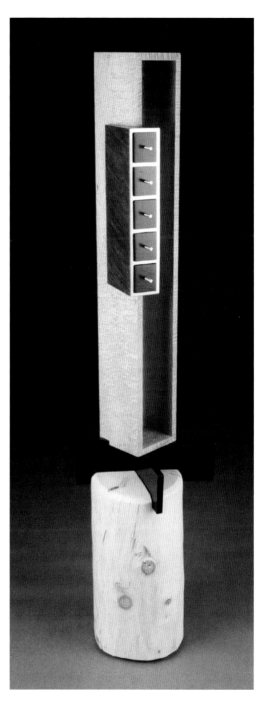

Cory Robinson
Flossy | 2007
58 X 14 X 15 INCHES (147.3 X 35.6 X 38.1 CM)
Curly maple, white pine, walnut,
poplar, aluminum, paint, gold leaf
PHOTO BY ARTIST

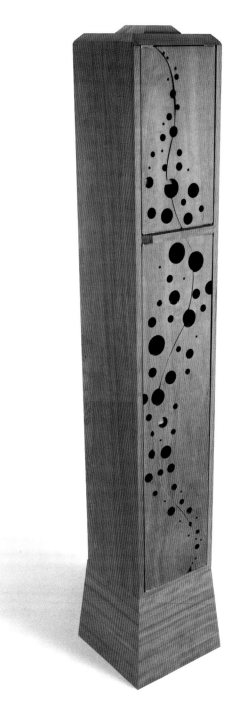
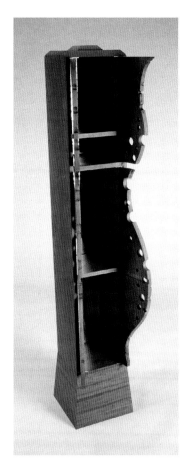

Kyle Capicik

Bubbles | 2008

66 X 10¼ X 10¼ INCHES (167.6 X 26 X 26 CM)

Padauk, purpleheart, Baltic birch plywood, mirror, acrylic paint

PHOTOS BY ARTIST

R. Thomas Tedrowe, Jr.
Myers Cabinet | 1998
62 X 22 X 16 INCHES (157.5 X 55.9 X 40.6 CM)
Makore, ebonized Honduran mahogany, macassar
ebony, curly maple, black coral, silver wire
PHOTOS BY ARTIST

Cosmo Barbaro

Jeanie | 2008

75 X 36 X 18 INCHES (190.5 X 91.4 X 45.7 CM)

Fiddleback mahogany, rosewood, maple, wenge, polished chrome hardware

PHOTO BY ARTIST

Martin Lane

Bubinga Humidor | 2001

51¼ X 16½ X 16½ INCHES (130.2 X 41.9 X 41.9 CM)

Bubinga, kerosingo, Belize cedar, ebony, glass, silver, satin matte lacquer

PHOTO BY BLANTERN & DAVIS LIMITED

James Esworthy
Untitled | 2007
26 X 78 X 18 INCHES (66 X 198.1 X 45.7 CM)

Glass, fabric, pecan burl, quartersawn mahogany,
dyed black inlay, brass, oil and polyurethane finish

PHOTOS BY KEN MAYER

Rhea Giffin

Where the Heart Is | 2005

20 X 22 X 14 INCHES (50.8 X 55.9 X 35.6 CM)

Papier-mâché, cellulose, found wooden
birdhouse, wire, epoxy, acrylic, polyurethane

PHOTO BY ARTIST

Timothy Maddox
Just Another Bandsaw Box | 2005
32 X 16 X 14 INCHES (81.3 X 40.6 X 35.6 CM)
Salvaged pine, steel, patina, paint
PHOTO BY BRENT SKIDMORE

Craig Thibodeau

Diamond Cabinet | 2008

34 X 42 X 20 INCHES (86.4 X 106.7 X 50.8 CM)

Jatoba, madrone burl, quartersawn maple, sapele

PHOTO BY CRAIG CARLSON

John Kaufmann
Little Sister | 2008
21½ X 10⅜ X 8¼ INCHES (54.6 X 26.4 X 21 CM)
Cherry, ebonized beech, shellac

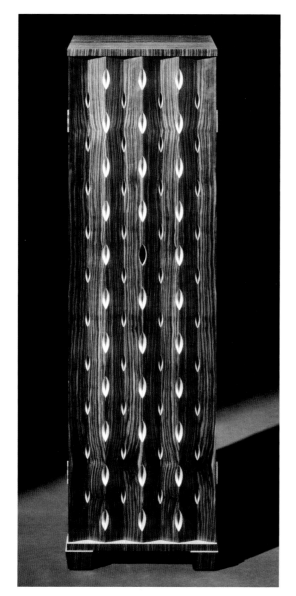

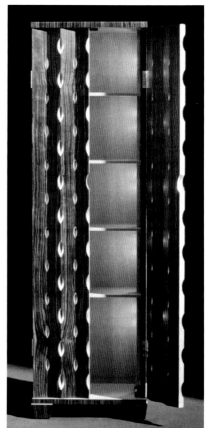

Gregg Lipton

Wizard Curio Cabinet | 2003

59 X 18 X 13 INCHES (149.9 X 45.7 X 33 CM)

Macassar ebony, Swiss pear, silver leaf with patina, oil varnish

PHOTOS BY DENNIS GRIGGS

Julia Bonnell

Henry Credenza | 2008

32 X 67 X 16 INCHES (81.3 X 170.2 X 33 CM)

Walnut, linseed oil, varathane finish

PHOTO BY ARTIST

Jack Reynolds

C.S.T. Credenza | 2008

24 X 48 X 20 INCHES (61 X 121.9 X 50.8 CM)

Oregon black walnut, spalted alder, ebony, tung oil, shellac

PHOTO BY ARTIST

Rich Soborowicz

Lingerie Cabinet | 2007

71 X 30 X 18¼ INCHES (180.3 X 76.2 X 46.4 CM)

Beech, cherry, English elm burl, rosewood, lacquer

PHOTO BY ARTIST

Paul Baines
Greene and Greene-Style Cherry CD Cabinet
with Bookmatched Cherry Veneer Doors | 2006
62¹⁄₄ X 30 X 11 INCHES (158.1 X 76.2 X 27.9 CM)
Cherry, steel, copper, polyurethane, plastic CD racks
PHOTO BY JOEL BUTKOWSKI

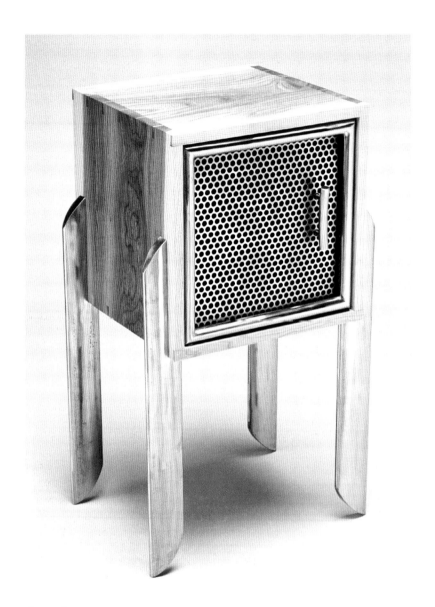

Arnt Arntzen

End Table | 2001

28 X 16 X 16 INCHES (71.1 X 40.6 X 40.6 CM)

Elm, steel, copper grounding rod, oval
bridge support, varathane, lacquer

PHOTO BY GORAN BASARIC

Jay T. Scott

Wall Cabinet for Geneviéve | 2005

24 X 18 X 6 INCHES (60.9 X 45.7 X 15.2 CM)

Kwila, maple, brass, gold leaf, shellac, wax

PHOTOS BY AARON BARNA

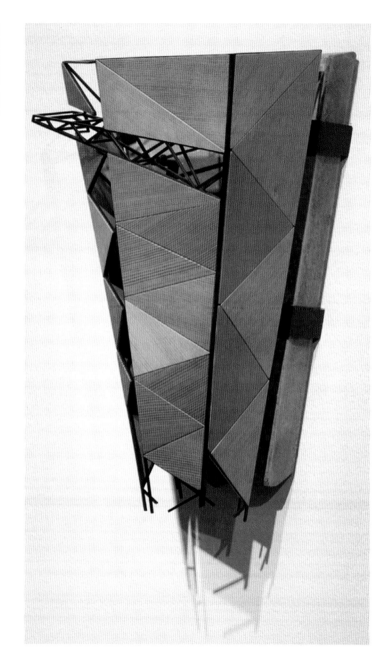

Marcus Papay
Facade | 2008
24 X 14 X 8 INCHES (60.9 X 35.5 X 20.3 CM)
Douglas fir, steel
PHOTOS BY ARTIST

Scott Grove

Amber | 2005

32 X 32 X 16 INCHES (81.3 X 81.3 X 40.6 CM)

Quilted maple, amber, silver, steam-bent oak, medium
density fiberboard, copper polychrome finish

PHOTO BY JOHN SMILLIE

Karen Ernst

Botanical Objects Cabinet | 2007

19 X 16 X 8 INCHES (48.3 X 40.6 X 20.3 CM)

Cherry, maple, mahogany, milk paint, varnish

PHOTOS BY ARTIST

Brad Smith
Green Skirt Cabinet | 2008
34 X 42 X 20 INCHES (86.4 X 106.7 X 50.8 CM)
Walnut, cherry, reclaimed painted beadboard,
charred cherry, comic strip transfers
PHOTO BY MICHAEL O'NEILL

George Beland
Untitled | 2009
54 X 36 X 22 INCHES (137.2 X 91.4 X 55.9 CM)
Birch, aniline dye, bronze, lacquer
PHOTO BY PERRY SMITH

Chad Aldridge
Hot out of the Oven | 2009
62 X 39 X 20 INCHES (157.4 X 99 X 50.8 CM)
Steel, lead, aluminum, rubber,
maple, enamel wash
PHOTO BY ARTIST

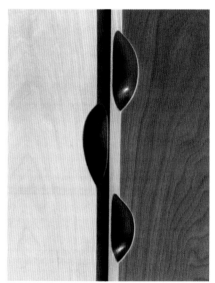

David Tragen

Fireland Flow | 2003

27½ X 16 X 9½ INCHES (69.9 X 40.6 X 24.1 CM)

Lenga, padauk

PHOTOS BY NORMAN YOUNG

Om Anand

Malone Display Cabinet | 2004

80 X 45 X 14 INCHES (203.2 X 114.3 X 35.6 CM)

Monterey cypress, madrone,
Port Orford cedar, glass, shellac

PHOTO BY PATRICK TREGENZA

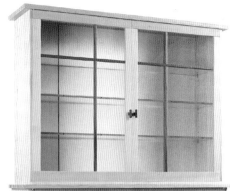

Todd Plummer

Tool Box | 2000

19¼ X 33½ X 15½ INCHES (48.9 X 85.1 X 39.4 CM)

Cherry, maple, shellac, wax

PHOTO BY ARTIST

Federico Méndez-Castro
Claro Cabinet | 2006
85 X 15 X 6 INCHES (215.9 X 38.1 X 15.2 CM)
Claro walnut, wenge, Spanish cedar,
mahogany, yew, shellac, wax
PHOTOS BY INGEBORG SUZANNE

Yoav S. Liberman
Attn: John Everdell | 2007
60 X 32 X 22 INCHES (152.4 X 81.3 X 55.9 CM)
Cedar, pine, cherry, fir, sapele, cotton-
linen fabric, milk paint, brass, steel
PHOTO BY ARTIST

Richard Judd

Tower Cabinet | 1995

72 X 20 X 12 INCHES (182.9 X 50.8 X 30.5 CM)

Birch plywood, maple, padauk, purpleheart, sycamore, amarello, anigre, ebonized poplar veneers, poplar, gold leaf, black lacquer, lacquer

PHOTO BY BILL LEMKE

Justin Kramer

Wine Cabinet | 2008

64 X 17 X 6 INCHES (162.6 X 43.2 X 15.2 CM)

Bloodwood, leather, dyed poplar, hard maple, birch plywood, zebrawood, zebrawood veneer, oil finish

PHOTOS BY ARTIST

Bill Barrand

Cone Leg Highboy | 1989

55 X 35 X 21½ INCHES (139.7 X 88.9 X 54.6 CM)

Padauk, figured maple, oil finish

PHOTO BY ARTIST

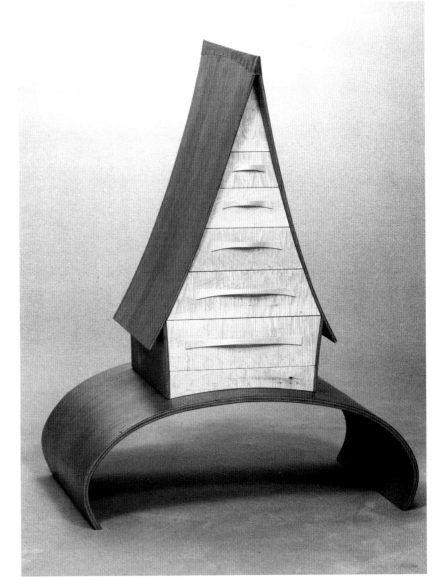

Paulus Wanrooij

Pagoda Cabinet | 2001

47 X 36 X 22 INCHES (119.4 X 91.4 X 55.9 CM)

Mahogany, curly maple, red oak

PHOTOS BY ARTIST

Trevor Doig

Geisha Cabinet | 2007

69 X 30 X 14 INCHES (175.3 X 76.2 X 35.6 CM)

Cherry, glass, aged brass hardware, oil finish

PHOTO BY ARTIST

Edward Wohl

Jewelry Cabinet | 2006

13 X 22 X 16 INCHES (33 X 55.9 X 40.6 CM)

Bird's-eye maple

PHOTOS BY AL LADA

Bobby Brinton
Redwood Wine Cabinet | 2008
30 X 28 INCHES (76.2 X 71.1 CM)
Reclaimed old-growth redwood
fence posts, found metal parts
PHOTOS BY ARTIST

Jordan Goodman
VAULTable | 2004
17 X 38 X 38 INCHES (43.2 X 96.5 X 96.5 CM)
Cherry, walnut, lacquer
PHOTOS BY ARTIST

Wells Mason

Big Black | 2008

25 X 100 X 20 INCHES (63.5 X 254 X 50.8 CM)

Formaldehyde-free medium density fiberboard, catalyzed
lacquer, steel, black patina, European-style hardware

PHOTO BY JIM TOBAC

Rosario Mercado
Untitled | 2002
60 X 14 X 12 INCHES (152.4 X 35.6 X 30.5 CM)
Poplar, graphite, silk, wire, stainless steel rod, glass
PHOTO BY PATRICIA MERCADO

Peter Dellert

Mariposa Liquor Cabinet | 2004

37 X 46 X 8 INCHES (94 X 116.8 X 20.3 CM)

Spalted maple, dyed curly maple,
quartersawn sycamore, ebonized cherry

PHOTO BY JOHN POLAK

Katie McLaughlin

Are You Sure? | 2009

28½ X 18 X 7 INCHES (72.4 X 45.7 X 17.8 CM)

Ash, poplar, painted medium density fiberboard, glass, brass, eggs, wire, painted hammer, polyester

PHOTOS BY ARTIST

Don Miller
Bow Front | 2006
52 X 22 X 8 INCHES (132.1 X 55.9 X 20.3 CM)
White oak, wax, silver
PHOTOS BY MARK JOHNSTON

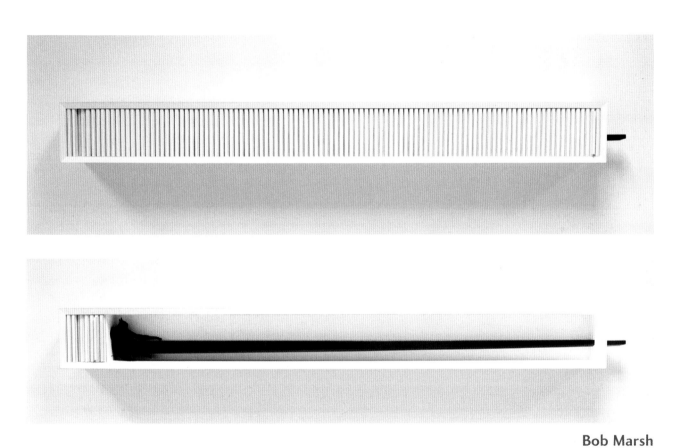

Bob Marsh

Sequence | 2008

7 X 65 X 7 INCHES (17.8 X 165.1 X 17.8 CM)

Wood, cast resin, paint

PHOTOS BY ARTIST

Alison J. McLennan
Chapman Building Cabinet | 2004
60 X 30 X 15 INCHES (152.4 X 76.2 X 38.1 CM)
Wood, oil and enamel paint, steel, copper,
lamp parts, clock
PHOTO BY ARTIST

Derek Chalfant

Blue-Eyed Chest | 2007

35½ X 20 X 19 INCHES (90.2 X 50.8 X 48.3 CM)

Curly cherry, ebony, bronze,
patina, blue eyes granite

PHOTO BY ARTIST

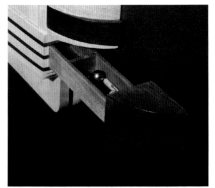

Glenn Paculba

Double Down the Line | 2001

48 X 24 X 5 INCHES (121.9 X 61 X 12.7 CM)

Maple, mahogany, acrylic plastic

PHOTOS BY MICHAEL JAMES

John Wiggers

Gentleman's Semainaire | 2003

52¾ X 25 X 25 INCHES (134 X 63.5 X 63.5 CM)

Curly bird's-eye maple, plywood, makore, mahogany, narra, maple, ebony, padauk, sycamore, satinwood, leather, satin nickel, polyurethane finish

PHOTOS BY JOHN GLOS

Greg Smith

Blanket Chest | 2008

19 X 22 X 34 INCHES (48.3 X 55.9 X 86.4 CM)

Teak, afzelia, copper, oil varnish, patina

PHOTO BY JOHN BIRCHARD

Mason McBrien

Sylvan Shimmer | 2008

37 X 35 X 18 INCHES (94 X 88.9 X 45.7 CM)

Curly hard maple, blister maple, black walnut, shellac

PHOTOS BY JIM DUGAN

Thomas Starbuck Stockton

Vienna Sideboard | 2008

60 X 15 X 36 INCHES (152.4 X 38.1 X 91.4 CM)

Curly maple, ebony, mother-of-pearl, tagua nut

PHOTO BY STEPHEN KIRKISH

Joy Umali
Specimen Cabinet | 2008
19½ X 16 X 9½ INCHES (49.5 X 40.6 X 24.1 CM)
Reclaimed elm, reclaimed walnut, salvaged
catalog pulls, cork, beeswax finish

PHOTOS BY MARK SERR

Shaun Fleming

Wall Cabinet with Cascading Mango Marquetry | 2003

18 X 16 X 9½ INCHES (45.7 X 40.6 X 24.1 CM)

Koa, plywood, cherry, mahogany, mango, lacquer

PHOTO BY ROB RATKOWSKI

Tom Calhoun

Ulu `Ohe (Bamboo Stand) | 2001

36 X 14 X 10 INCHES (91.4 X 35.6 X 25.4 CM)

Curly koa, curly mango, Nigerian satinwood, Chinese
marble, brass knife hinges, oil/varnish finish

PHOTO BY XINIA PRODUCTIONS

Lynn Szymanski
Untitled | 2005
13 X 12 X 7 INCHES (33 X 30.5 X 17.8 CM)
Plywood, walnut veneer, poplar,
building blocks, paint
PHOTO BY UNH PHOTOGRAPHIC SERVICES

Wendy Maruyama
*You Don't Know What
You've Got 'til It's Gone
(Memorial to the Tasmanian Tiger)* | 2003
50 X 15 X 12 INCHES (127 X 38.1 X 30.5 CM)
Mahogany, milk paint, video, lead, fur, nails
PHOTOS BY MICHAEL SLATTERY

Katie Hudnall

Sea Sloom | 2009

34 X 60 X 16 INCHES (86.4 X 152.4 X 40.6 CM)

Plywood, found/reclaimed hardwoods, glass, copper, found castor, paint, ink, colored pencil, lacquer, wax

PHOTOS BY TAYLOR DABNEY

Vincent Leman

Stacked Cabinet No. 5 | 2008

59 X 24 X 16 INCHES (149.9 X 61 X 40.6 CM)

Birch plywood, acrylic paint, urethane

PHOTO BY ARTIST

Curt Minier

Sideboard | 2008

33½ X 72 X 24 INCHES (85.1 X 182.9 X 61 CM)

Beech, colored lacquer, glass top, colored foils

PHOTO BY GREG KROGSTAD

Todd Sorenson
Bedside Cabinet | 2006
29 X 20 X 14 INCHES (73.7 X 50.8 X 35.6 CM)
Jarrah, Swiss pear, western maple
PHOTO BY JOHN BIRCHARD

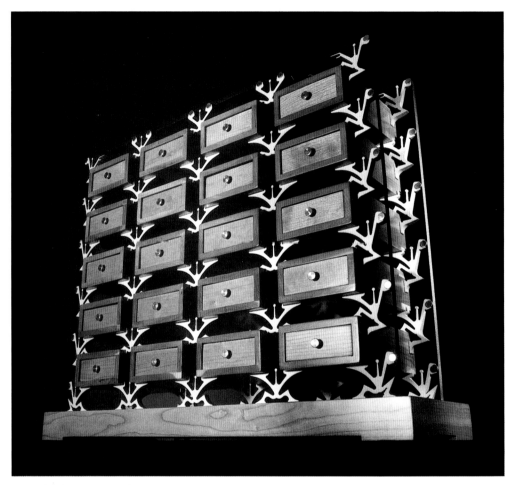

Mordechai Schleifer

The Sultan's Treasures | 2000

22 X 28 X 8 INCHES (55.9 X 71.1 X 20.3 CM)

Cherry, aluminum

PHOTO BY JONATHAN RACHLINE

Daniella Peña
Elevate | 2005
70 X 12 X 12 INCHES (177.8 X 30.5 X 30.5 CM)
Birch plywood, aluminum,
concrete, glass, oil varnish, paint
PHOTO BY ARTIST

Yuri Kobayashi

Nascence | 2005

56 X 18 X 18 INCHES (142.2 X 45.7 X 45.7 CM)

Hard maple, aluminum, water

PHOTOS BY LARRY STANLEY

John Lee

Farraige | 2008

36 X 84 X 29 INCHES (91.4 X 213.4 X 73.7 CM)

European white oak, European
lime, leather, acrylic lacquer

Don Brasseaux

Ghormely Hutch | 2008

72 X 36 X 13 INCHES (182.9 X 91.4 X 33 CM)

Salvaged cypress and pine

PHOTO BY ARTIST

Marc Fish

Milburn Cabinet with Drawer | 2008

83 X 30 X 30 INCHES (210.8 X 76.2 X 76.2 CM)

Macassar ebony, rippled sycamore, glass,
African ebony, brass hinges, shellac polish, wax

PHOTOS BY ARTIST

Paul Schürch

The Rose Chest | 2005

34 X 46½ X 21½ INCHES (86.4 X 118.1 X 54.6 CM)

Mahogany, imbuya burl, tulip, poplar, jade, opal, malachite, lapis lazuli, turquoise

PHOTOS BY WAYNE MCCALL

Wyatt Severs
Untitled | 2009

68 X 35 X 27 INCHES (172.7 X 88.9 X 68.6 CM)

Cherry, maple, poplar, plywood,
milk paint, copper, boxwood

PHOTO BY ROBERT GIESE

221

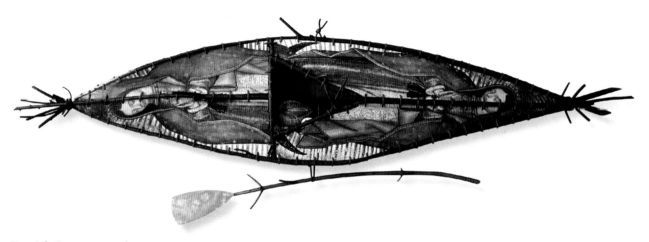

David Greenwood

Para los Mayas (Reliquary Cabinet) | 2007

29 X 86 X 8 INCHES (73.7 X 218.4 X 20.3 CM)

Sassafras, collaged paper, leather, stain, found seashells

PHOTO BY ARTIST

Thomas Throop

Colebrook Cabinet | 2000

48 X 25 X 25 INCHES (121.9 X 63.5 X 63.5 CM)

Walnut, plum pudding mahogany,
holly inlay, oil, wax

PHOTO BY FRANK POOLE

Myrl Phelps

Chinese Coffer | 2008

30 X 36 X 22 INCHES (76.2 X 91.4 X 55.8 CM)

Cherry, quartersawn sycamore, custom brass hardware

PHOTO BY JIM DUGAN

Roger Heitzman
Nouveau Buffet | 2000
90 X 90 X 30 INCHES (228.6 X 228.6 X 76.2 CM)
Mahogany, granite, glass, cast bronze
PHOTO BY ARTIST

Norman Pirollo

Twin Plumes | 2009

55 X 26 X 13½ INCHES (139.7 X 66 X 34.3 CM)

European beech, mahogany, alder, cocobolo, shellac, wax

PHOTOS BY LINDA CHENARD

Jeff Trigg
Stereo Console | 2005
28 X 59¹/₂ X 15 INCHES (71.1 X 151.1 X 38.1 CM)
Western bigleaf maple, Western red
cedar, black walnut, oil/varnish mixture
PHOTO BY KEN MAYER

William Laberge

Player-Piano Roll Cabinet | 2007

53 X 63 X 19 INCHES (134.6 X 160 X 48.3 CM)

Cherry, quilted maple, walnut

PHOTO BY JOHN CONTE

Steve Holman
S&P Semainier and Stool | 2007
76 X 26 X 26 INCHES (193 X 66 X 66 CM)
Curly maple, purpleheart, negal,
quartersawn mahogany, lacquer
PHOTO BY JOHN CONTE

J-P Vilkman
Composition #1 | 1999

58 X 40 X 16 INCHES (147.3 X 101.6 X 40.6 CM)

Yellowheart, bloodwood, wenge, ebony, canary wood

PHOTO BY SETH JANOFSKY

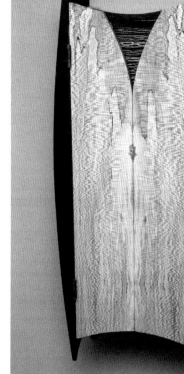

Michael Hoffer
Cholla Cabinet | 2003

30 X 13 X 5½ INCHES (76.2 X 33 X 14 CM)

Quartersawn sycamore, dyed white oak,
bird's-eye maple, cholla cactus sticks

PHOTO BY JAMES HART

Leah Woods

Bespoke: Cabinet for a Gentleman's Shoes | 2008

43 X 58 X 22 INCHES (109.2 X 147.3 X 55.9 CM)

White oak, stainless steel hardware, black dye, oil varnish

PHOTOS BY DEAN POWELL

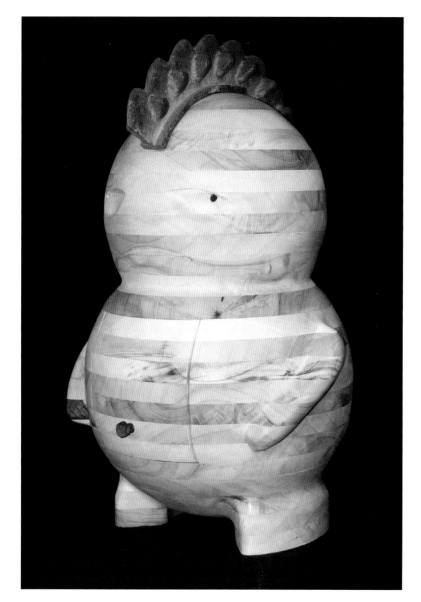

Sean Favero

Creature | 2009

23 X 17 X 15 INCHES (58.4 X 43.2 X 38.1 CM)

Poplar, reclaimed steel, LED light, tung oil

PHOTOS BY ARTIST

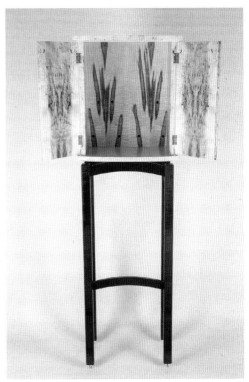

Thomas Elsner Smith
The Giving Tree | 2008
56 X 18 X 12 INCHES (142.2 X 45.7 X 30.5 CM)
Maple
PHOTOS BY ARTIST

Marc Fish

Milburn Japanese Cabinet | 2008

51 X 16 X 11 INCHES (129.5 X 40.6 X 27.9 CM)

Macassar ebony, rippled sycamore, glass,
French polish finish, sterling silver plaque

PHOTO BY ARTIST

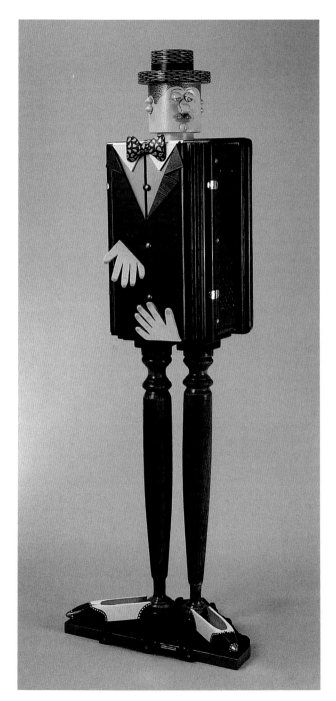

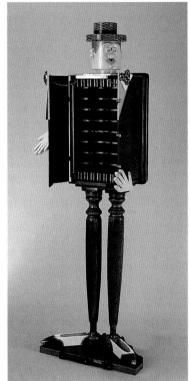

Penny Weinstein
Corafton Winthrop IV | 1995
58 X 19 X 14 INCHES (147.3 X 48.3 X 35.6 CM)
Sewing machine case, foundry patterns,
wooden found objects, acrylic paint
PHOTOS BY ROBERT RATTNER

Steven Henderson
Untitled | 2006
9 X 30 X 11 INCHES (22.9 X 76.2 X 27.9 CM)
Walnut, redwood, pine
PHOTO BY TOBIN GRIMSHAW

Brent Skidmore
Bumple Brown Pair | 2008
28 X 28 X 28 INCHES
(71.1 X 71.1 X 71.1 CM)
Walnut, maple, poplar, mahogany,
acrylic paint, glass
PHOTO BY MICHAEL TRAISTER

Justin Dehner

2 x Used | 2008

19¾ X 60 X 20 INCHES (50.1 X 152.4 X 50.8 CM)

Glass, pallet wood, steel

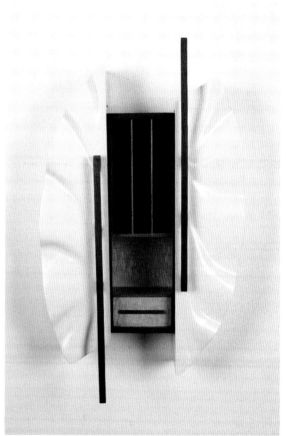

Mark Boston
Wave Cabinet | 2008
30 X 12 X 5 INCHES (76.2 X 30.5 X 12.7 CM)
Cocobolo, poplar, orange agate, mappa burl veneer,
polycrylic finish, latex paint, aluminum tubing
PHOTOS BY ARTIST

Martin Tatarka

Glaze Formulating Table | 2007

34 X 90 X 23 INCHES (86.4 X 228.6 X 58.4 CM)

Plywood, paint, hardware

PHOTO BY ARTIST

Dustin Farnsworth and Eric Britton

Jug | 2007

32 X 24 X 20 INCHES (81.3 X 61 X 50.8 CM)

Mild steel, high-density polyethylene, hardware

PHOTO BY PETER MCDANIEL

Dudley Mack
13th Floor | 2008
120 X 24 X 12 INCHES (304.8 X 61 X 30.5 CM)
Teak veneer, solid teak, particleboard
PHOTO BY ARTIST

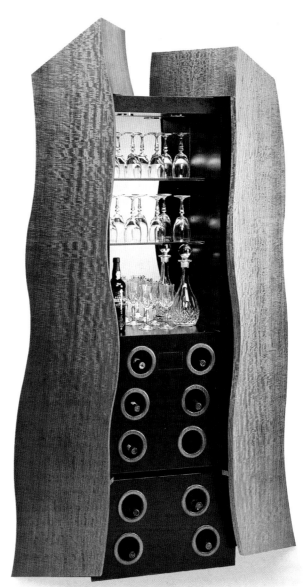

John Wiggers

Andiroba Wine Cabinet | 1998

84 X 32 X 19 INCHES (213.4 X 81.3 X 48.3 CM)

Bee's-wing andiroba, plywood, nero assolute
 granite, cherry, glass, mirror, polyurethane finish

PHOTOS BY JOHN GLOS

John Lee

Scully | 2003

EACH, 63 X 18 X 18 INCHES (160 X 45.7 X 45.7 CM)

Maple, figured sycamore, madrone burr, polyurethane lacquer

PHOTO BY JAMES DELANEY

Jacques Breau
Showcase Cabinet | 2007
48 X 26 X 13 INCHES (121.9 X 66 X 33 CM)
Spalted Western maple, brown doussie, Port
Orford cedar, brass, glass, oil finish, shellac, wax
PHOTO BY INGEBORG SUZANNE

Ryan Seiler

Cabinetmaker's Cabinet | 2008

59 X 21 X 12 INCHES (149.9 X 53.3 X 30.5 CM)

Cherry, walnut, spalted maple, mahogany, oak, catalpa, unidentified wood, shellac

PHOTO BY GEORGE ENSLEY

Timothy Maddox
Nilla Nanna | 2006
34 X 34 X 18 INCHES (86.4 X 86.4 X 45.7 CM)
Steel, alder, patina, paint, lacquer
PHOTO BY ARTIST

Juan Carlos Fernandez

Zulu | 2007

18 X 11 X 5 INCHES (45.7 X 27.9 X 12.7 CM)

Bubinga, pear, Eastern maple, plum, palisander

PHOTOS BY RAQUEL FORS

Josh Judge
Pandora's Box | 2009
13 X 13 X 5 INCHES (33 X 33 X 12.7 CM)
Sydney blue gum, African wenge,
palisander, Scandinavian oil, leather
PHOTOS BY MICHAEL FORTUNE AND ARTIST

Seth Rolland

Charis Credenza | 2007

36 X 64 X 23 INCHES (91.4 X 162.6 X 58.4 CM)

Walnut, maple, curly maple

PHOTOS BY FRANK ROSS

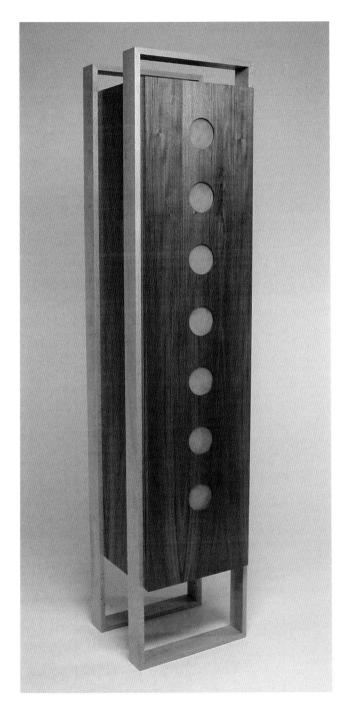

Ross Thompson

Wine Cabinet | 2008

79 X 18 X 17½ INCHES (200.7 X 45.7 X 44.5 CM)

Beech, walnut, glass, lacquer

PHOTOS BY ARTIST

Kent Perdue
Rink | 2009
67½ X 11 X 5 INCHES (171.5 X 27.9 X 12.7 CM)
Pine, mahogany, brass, Purple Heart medal
PHOTOS BY ARTIST

Patrick Griffin Downes

Lola's Jewelry Mansion | 2009

51 X 24 X 16 INCHES (129.5 X 61 X 40.6 CM)

Salvaged birch and maple; reclaimed
walnut, recycled fiber, graphite, oil, wax

PHOTO BY JIM DUGAN

Ross Annels

Helena's Cabinet | 2008

38 X 96 X 25 INCHES (96.5 X 243 X 63 CM)

Silky oak, hoop pine plywood, aluminum, oil finish

PHOTO BY ARTIST

Kevin-Louis Barton

Chopstick Shrine | 2004

12¹/₂ X 6 X 4 INCHES (31.8 X 15.2 X 10.2 CM)

Mahogany, fabric, steel hinges,
bamboo chopsticks, ceramic teacup

PHOTOS BY ARTIST

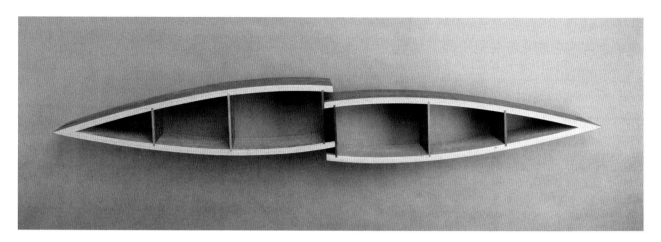

Lauren Manuel

Disjoined Canoe | 2007

7¼ X 53⅛ X 6¾ INCHES (19.7 X 135.6 X 17.1 CM)

Baltic birch, walnut, cherry veneer, Danish oil

PHOTO BY ARTIST

Russell Gale

The Garboard Strake | 2009

34 X 52 X 17 INCHES (86.4 X 132.1 X 43.2 CM)

Black limba, sen, sassafrass, various
substrates, brass, shellac, wax

PHOTO BY DAVID WELTER

Christina Pupo
TV Cabinet | 2008
27 X 41 X 15 INCHES (68.6 X 104.1 X 38.1 CM)
Bamboo veneer, greenboard, solid
butternut, linseed oil, beeswax
PHOTO BY ARTIST

Steve Ogle

Red Box | 2005

36½ X 64 X 21 INCHES (92.7 X 162.6 X 53.3 CM)

Charred ash, dyed maple, copper, lacquer

PHOTO BY CRAIG MURPHY PHOTOGRAPHY

Dustin Farnsworth

Menagerie | 2008

52 X 16 X 16 INCHES (132.1 X 40.6 X 40.6 CM)

Poplar, walnut, steel, canvas, string, latex
paint, toned lacquer, satin lacquer

PHOTO BY PETER MCDANIEL

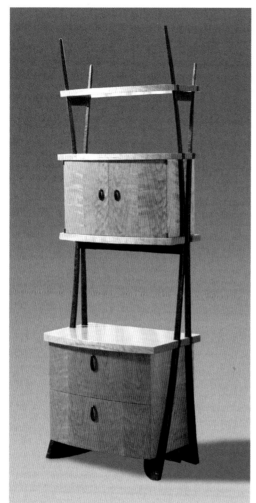

Rob Hare

Narrow Sideboard | 2005

84 X 30 X 20 INCHES (213.4 X 76.2 X 50.8 CM)

Figured cherry, maple, wenge, forged steel

PHOTO BY CHRIS KENDALL

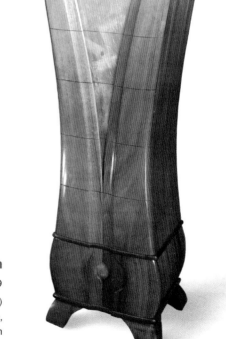

Tom Christenson

Untitled | 2009

63 X 26 X 14 INCHES (160 X 66 X 35.6 CM)

Mahogany, gold leaf, crackle,
acrylic, maple, oil/varnish finish

PHOTO BY ARTIST

Stefan During

Tall Chest | 2003

87 X 26 X 12 INCHES (221 X 30.5 X 66 CM)

Maple, apple, glass

PHOTO BY ARTIST

Joel Green

Hoover's Closet | 2007

72 X 21 X 25 INCHES (182.9 X 53.3 X 63.5 CM)

African mahogany, brass, mirror

PHOTOS BY MARK JOHNSTON

Isaac Arms
Toothbrush Vanity Crank Box | 2003
27 X 25 X 10 INCHES (68.6 X 63.5 X 25.4 CM)
Mahogany, maple, cherry, steel, glass, milk paint
PHOTOS BY BILL LEMKE

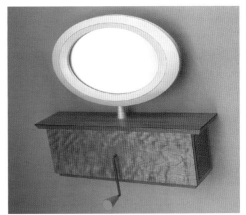

Paul Schürch

The Ribbon High Cabinet | 2006

72½ X 36 X 21 INCHES (184.2 X 91.4 X 53.3 CM)

Walnut, Swiss pear, satinwood

PHOTO BY WAYNE MCCALL

Lord Godfrey

Teak Sideboard 01 | 2007

35 X 45 X 15 INCHES (88.9 X 114.3 X 38.1 CM)

Teak, beech, bocote, oil

PHOTO BY INGEBORG SUZANNE

Ricardo Vasquez

Untitled | 2003

32 X 72 X 18 INCHES (81.3 X 182.9 X 45.7 CM)

Mahogany, wenge, glass, stainless
steel, conversion varnish

PHOTO BY ARTIST

Debra Johansen
Stanley Johansen
Untitled | 2009

15 X 7 X 4 INCHES (38.1 X 17.8 X 10.2 CM)
Rosewood, old glass factory box, roof copper, acrylic
paint, brass, handmade earthenware knobs

PHOTOS BY KRISTYN NORDSTROM PHOTOGRAPHY

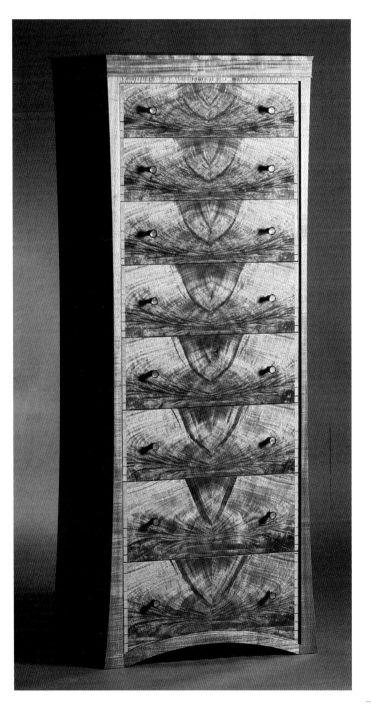

Neil Erasmus

Sylvia | 1997

59 X 22⁷/₈ X 19 INCHES (149.9 X 58.1 X 48.3 CM)

Tasmanian blackwood, celery-top pine,
cedar of Lebanon, pigskin suede

PHOTOS BY EVAN COLLIS

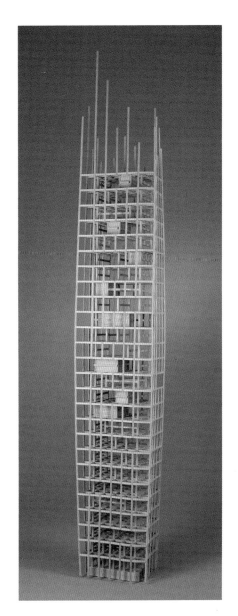

Yuri Kobayashi

Being | 2005

108 X 17 X 14 INCHES (274.3 X 43.2 X 35.6 CM)

Ash

PHOTOS BY LARRY STANLEY

Rob Porcaro
Cabinet for CDs | 2003
34 X 8¹/₂ X 7¹/₂ INCHES (86.4 X 21.6 X 19.1 CM)
Spalted maple, mahogany, ebony,
shellac, wax, water-base acrylic, wax
PHOTO BY ARTIST

Margaret Polcawich
Abutilon Cabinet | 2003
24 X 17 X 7 INCHES (61 X 43.2 X 17.8 CM)
Cherry, walnut and maple veneer,
paint, polymer clay, copper
PHOTOS BY ARTIST

Penny Weinstein

Edgar Simonneau | 2000

65 X 19 X 15 INCHES (165.1 X 48.3 X 38.1 CM)

Wooden furniture, found objects, antique metal sign, antique bottle caps, sprinkler heads, scale number display, antique toy, acrylic paint

PHOTO BY ROBERT RATTNER

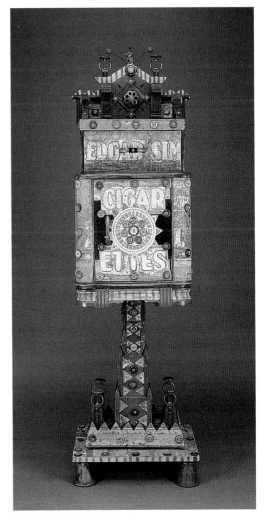

Graham Campbell

Drinking Cabinet | 1986

54 X 22 X 22 INCHES (137.2 X 55.9 X 55.9 CM)

Painted birch plywood, chipboard

PHOTO BY ARTIST

Joel Kresner

One-Off #356: Jewelry Box with
Bowl and Earrings | 2009

13½ X 14¾ X 9¾ INCHES (34.3 X 37.5 X 24.8 CM)

Purpleheart, black palm, curly
maple, verde aniline dye, ebonol

PHOTO BY ARTIST

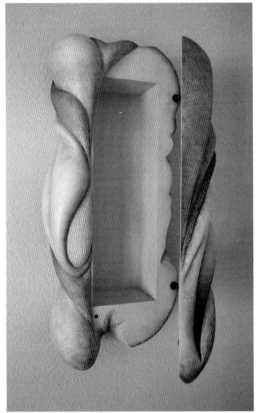

Yang Jun Kwon
My Loneliness II | 1997
22 X 9 X 7 INCHES (55.9 X 22.9 X 17.8 CM)
Basswood, acrylic paint
PHOTOS BY ARTIST

Ken Richards

Breakfront Showcase | 1999

74 X 42 X 17 INCHES (188 X 106.7 X 43.2 CM)

Figured Ceylon satinwood, ebony, brass, glass, oil/wax finish

Peter Loh
Kasbah | 2007
VARIOUS DIMENSIONS
Santos mahogany, maple, cocobolo,
glass, brass, oil varnish
PHOTOS BY ARTIST

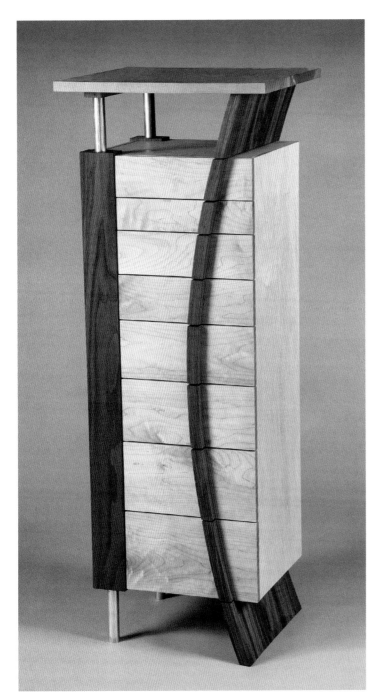

Robb Helmkamp

Biernbaum Jewelry Armoire | 2009

48 X 18 X 16 INCHES (121.9 X 45.7 X 40.6 CM)

Walnut, maple, aluminum

PHOTO BY TIM BARNWELL

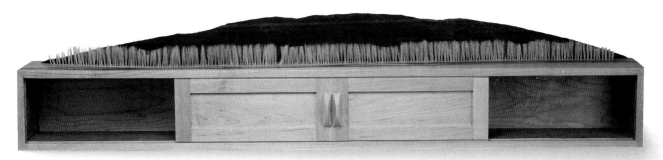

Oliver Percival
Untitled | 2009
6 X 48 X 6 INCHES (15.2 X 121.9 X 15.2 CM)
Maple, welded steel, nylon bristles
PHOTO BY JAY YORK

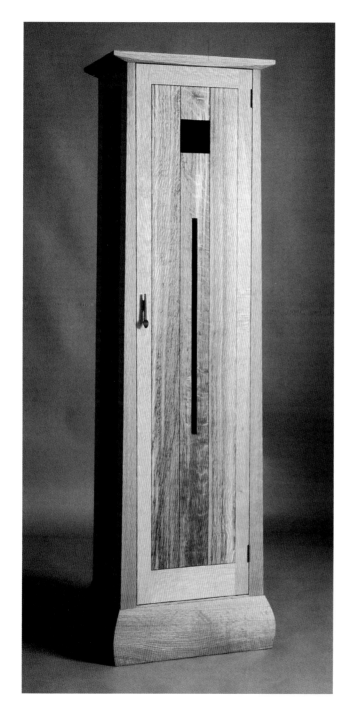

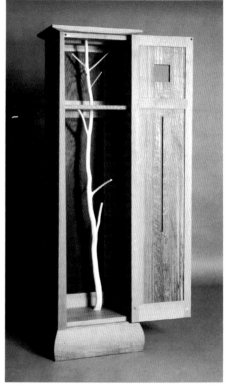

Thomas Throop

Centennial Cabinet | 2004

68 X 22 X 17 INCHES (172.7 X 55.9 X 43.2 CM)

White oak, English brown oak, bog oak, bleached oak sapling, oil, wax

PHOTOS BY ARTIST

Yang Jun Kwon
Untitled | 1994
74 X 30 X 19 INCHES (188 X 76.2 X 48.3 CM)
Mahogany
PHOTO BY ARTIST

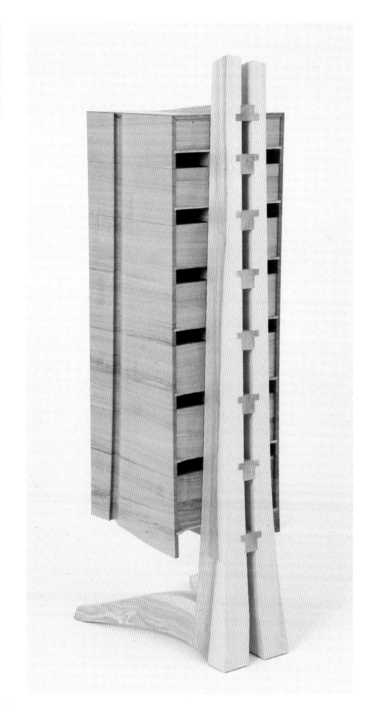

Daniel Lacey

Chestless | 2007

58 X 15 X 21 INCHES (147.3 X 38.1 X 53.3 CM)

Olive ash, cherry, British cedar of Lebanon

PHOTOS BY CLIVE PITTAM

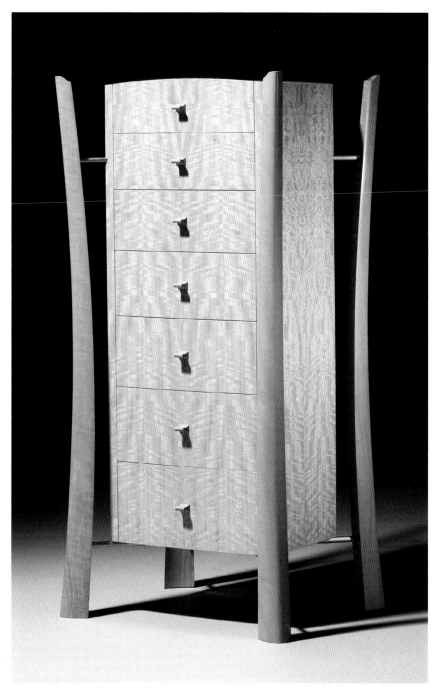

Brian Sargent
Lingerie Chest | 2008
44 X 22 X 19 INCHES (111.8 X 55.9 X 48.3 CM)
Mottled anigre, Swiss pear, hard maple,
stainless steel, oil varnish, satin lacquer
PHOTO BY BILL TRUSLOW

Adrian French
Cherry Case | 2004
45 X 30 X 16½ INCHES (114.3 X 76.2 X 41.9 CM)
Cherry
PHOTO BY ARTIST

Ted Lott
Square D Cabinet | 2007
18 X 10 X 7 INCHES (45.7 X 25.4 X 17.8 CM)
Recycled pine, found steel door, found objects
PHOTO BY ARTIST

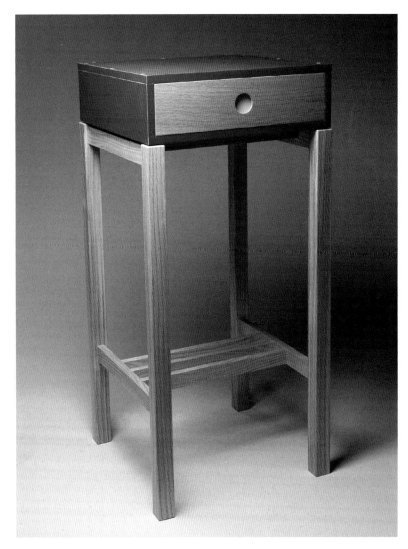

Matthew Nauman
Three for One | 2009
36½ X 17 X 17 INCHES (92.7 X 43.2 X 43.2 CM)
Oak, medium density fiberboard, milk paint
PHOTOS BY ARTIST

Heather DeLonga

Mr. Mania in Box Form | 2008

22 X 10 X 9 INCHES (55.9 X 25.4 X 22.9 CM)

Pine, poplar, cherry, walnut, bark, dowel rods, plywood

PHOTOS BY ARTIST

Theo Kamecke

Pharaoh's Secret | 1995

46 X 27 X 21 INCHES (116.8 X 68.6 X 53.3 CM)

Electronic circuitry boards, wood

Bailey Humbert Heck

Petrone Console | 2005

30 X 62 X 20 INCHES (76.2 X 157.5 X 50.8 CM)

American quartersawn cherry, polymerized
tung oil, 316 stainless steel, acid-etched
glass, natural gray cleft slate

PHOTO BY ARTIST

Justin Yasgoor

For Drawings | 2008

12 X 20 X 26 INCHES (30.5 X 50.8 X 66 CM)

Cypress walnut, wax

PHOTO BY MARK SERR

Tjeerd Hendel-Blackford
Winter's End Chest of Drawers | 2006
45 X 36 X 20 INCHES (114.3 X 91.4 X 50.8 CM)
Brown oak, pippy oak, cedar of
Lebanon, Danish oil, bison wax
PHOTO BY BRIAN J. BLACKFORD

Jeff O'Brien

Coopered Cabinet | 2007

24 X 12 X 9½ INCHES (61 X 30.5 X 24.1 CM)

Douglas fir, walnut, cherry

PHOTO BY ARTIST

Nicholas Chandler
Oak Bedside Cabinet | 2005
26 X 16 X 12 INCHES (66 X 40.6 X 30.5 CM)
American white oak
PHOTO BY ARTIST

Alf Sharp

McIntyre Chest-on-Chest | 2006

103 X 51 X 25 INCHES (261.6 X 129.5 X 63.5 CM)

Mahogany, gilded brass pulls

PHOTO BY JOHN LUCAS

Barry Daggett
Untitled | 2003
32 X 40 X 20 INCHES (81.3 X 101.6 X 50.8 CM)
Walnut, walnut crotch, maple, ebony
PHOTOS BY JOHN POLAK

William Laberge

Mettowee Huntboard | 2008

39 X 62 X 22 INCHES (99.1 X 157.5 X 55.9 CM)

Cherry, walnut, silver

PHOTO BY JOHN CONTE

William Laberge
Cloud Lift Desk | 2006
48 X 50 X 24 INCHES (121.9 X 127 X 61 CM)
Cherry, walnut, ebony
PHOTO BY ARTIST

Pat Megowan

Musician's Sideboard | 2005

55 X 16¼ X 32 INCHES (139.7 X 41.3 X 81.3 CM)

Honduran mahogany, rosewood, cocobolo, hard maple, sitka spruce, poplar, African blackwood, brass, varnish, shellac

PHOTOS BY JIM DUGAN

Kenneth Doppelt
Untitled | 2009
33 X 21 X 8 INCHES (83.8 X 53.3 X 20.3 CM)
Swiss pearwood, gel varnish
PHOTOS BY ELIZABETH LAMARK OF ETC PHOTO

Mitchell Pickard

Angeline Console | 2000

7 X 60 X 15 INCHES (17.8 X 152.4 X 38.1 CM)

Plywood, python-embossed leather,
stainless steel, polyurethane

PHOTO BY JOHN GLOS

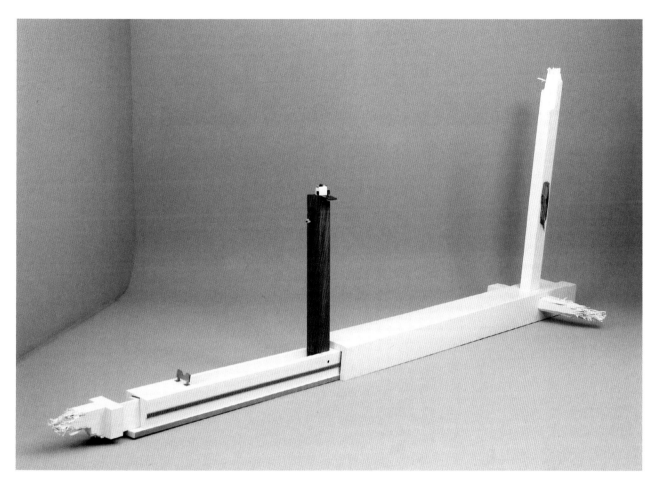

Adrian French

Abiding Fortune: Fragment 4 | 2006

74 X 21 X 168 INCHES (187.9 X 53.3 X 426.7 CM)

Painted medium density fiberboard, Douglas fir, plywood, mahogany, aluminum, iron, salvaged items, cast gold

PHOTO BY LARRY STANLEY

Juan Carlos Fernandez
Trinity | 2008
41 X 18 X 19 INCHES (104.1 X 45.7 X 48.3 CM)
Red cedar burl, mahogany,
Douglas fir, palisander
PHOTOS BY RAQUEL FORS

Frank De Jong
Walnut Preserve | 2008
34½ X 16¼ X 15 INCHES (87.6 X 41.3 X 39.4 CM)
Acrylic, walnut, red oak, linseed oil
PHOTO BY ARTIST

Angus Ross
Drinks Cabinet | 2008
43¼ X 25½ INCHES (109.9 X 64.8 CM)
Oak, wenge, glass lacquer
PHOTOS BY JULIE CAMPBELL

Ian Factor

Cantilevered Media Cabinet | 2007

24 X 72 X 16 INCHES (61 X 182.9 X 40.6 CM)

Birch plywood, Tasmanian bark veneer, black laminate

PHOTO BY ARTIST

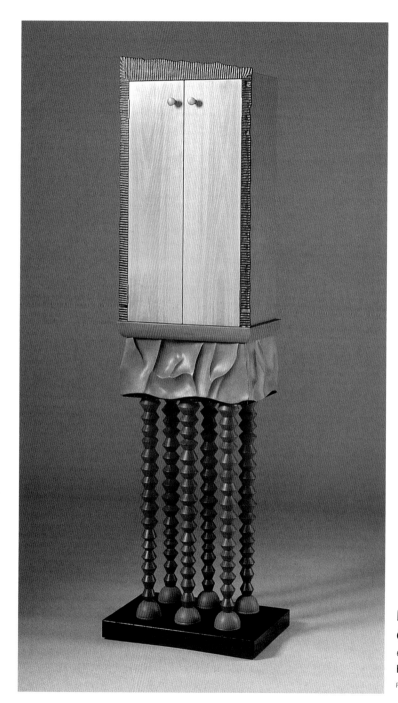

Michael Cullen
Girl Cabinet | 1996
63 X 15½ X 12 INCHES (160 X 39.4 X 30.5 CM)
Lemon wood, paint
PHOTO BY JOHN MCDONALD

Dale Lewis

Sighborgenus | 1997

84 X 36 X 16 INCHES (213.4 X 91.4 X 40.6 CM)

Maple, lacewood, purpleheart, poplar, lacquer finish

PHOTOS BY LEWIS KENNEDY

Leah Woods

Footloose and Fancy Free: A Showcase for Extraordinary Shoes | 2008

72 X 26 X 14 INCHES (182.9 X 66 X 35.6 CM)

Maple, anigre, brass hardware, shellac

PHOTOS BY DEAN POWELL

Declan O'Donoghue

Ripple Collector's Cabinet | 2007

94^{5}/$_{16}$ X 39^{1}/$_{4}$ X 21^{1}/$_{4}$ INCHES (239.6 X 99.7 X 54 CM)

Quilted maple, weathered sycamore, faux suede

PHOTO BY ARTIST

Matthew Werner
Moonflower Clock | 2006
60 X 12 X 8 INCHES (152.4 X 30.5 X 20.3 CM)
Jarrah, Western maple, wenge, brass with patina, epoxy, clock
mechanism, holly, orange, and iroko inlays, shellac, wax
PHOTO BY PAUL TITANGOS

Timothy Coleman
Yew and Me | 2003
60 X 32 X 14 INCHES (152.4 X 81.3 X 35.6 CM)
Western yew, English sycamore, imbuya, shellac
PHOTO BY CHARLEY FRIEBURG

Paul Henry

Federal Cabinet | 1997

68 X 21 X 14 INCHES (172.2 X 53.3 X 35.5 CM)

Salvaged oak, mahogany,
rubber, anigre, ebonized cherry

PHOTO BY DAVID HARRISON

Rob Hare

Stereo Cabinet | 2006

60 X 42 X 24 INCHES (152.4 X 106.7 X 61 CM)

Figured maple, hard maple, forged steel

PHOTO BY CHRIS KENDALL

Paul Schürch

Spin Cabinet | 2005

20 X 47½ INCHES (50.8 X 120.7 CM)

Cherry, myrtle burl, tulip, poplar
imbuya, purpleheart, maple, tulip

PHOTOS BY WAYNE MCCALL

Pat Scull

Butterfly Music/Jewelry Box | 2008

24 X 12 X 8 INCHES (61 X 30.5 X 20.3 CM)

Recycled wooden jewelry case, ceramic music box, ceramic
butterfly, glass, computer photos, sewing parts, ceramic
light box, wood legs, wood beads, sewing patterns

PHOTOS BY SETH TICE LEWIS

Michele Sommer Shapiro
Misery Is the River . . . Cabinet | 2006
14 X 8 X 3 INCHES (35.6 X 20.3 X 7.6 CM)
Pine, acrylic paint, plastic, ceramic doll parts, lace,
cut nails, twig, beads, staples, paper collage
PHOTO BY HAROLD SHAPIRO

Shaun Fleming
Mango Wood Chest of Drawers | 2000

30 X 52 X 22 INCHES (76.2 X 132 X 55.9 CM)

Koa, bending plywood, cherry,
mahogany, milo, mango, lacquer

PHOTO BY ROB RATKOWSKI

John Thoe

Bubbles (Wine Cabinet) | 1994

54 X 38 X 22 INCHES (137.2 X 96.5 X 55.9 CM)

Oregon walnut, Honduran mahogany

PHOTO BY ARTIST

Theo Kamecke

Zoroaster | 2005

8 X 17 X 13 INCHES (20.3 X 43.2 X 33 CM)

Electronic circuitry boards, wood

PHOTO BY ARTIST

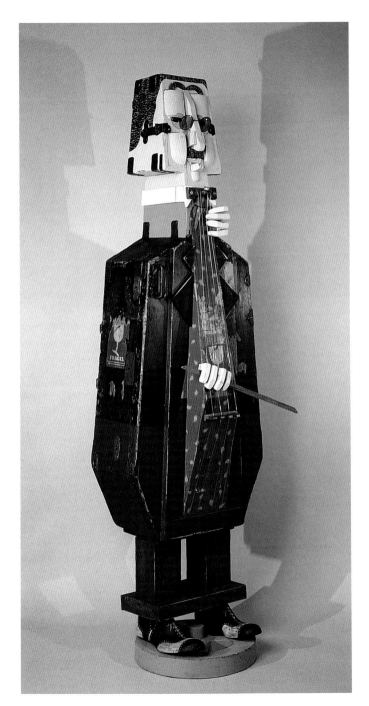

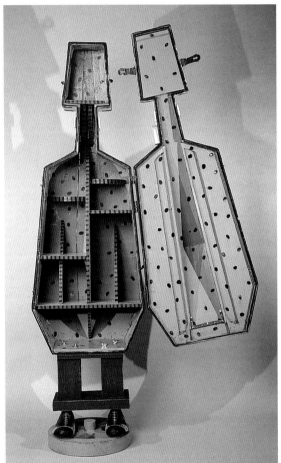

Penny Weinstein

Marcello | 1994

60 X 20 X 26 INCHES (152.4 X 50.8 X 66 CM)

Basswood, found wood, found
metal objects, acrylic paint

PHOTOS BY ROBERT RATTNER

Nick Allen

Stretched Colosseum | 2004

71 X 28 X 28 INCHES (180.3 X 71.1 X 71.1 CM)

Sycamore, figured ash, zebrano

PHOTO BY ARTIST

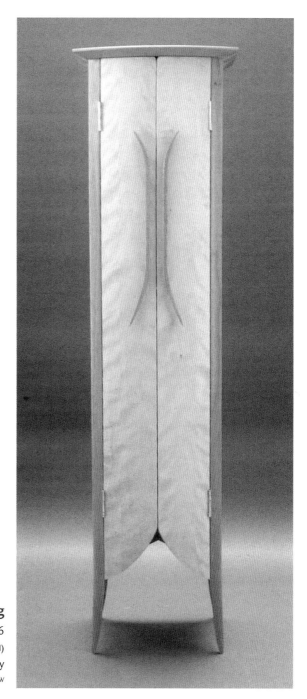

David Young

Lingerie Cabinet | 2006

54 X 13 X 15 INCHES (137.2 X 33 X 38.1 CM)

Flaming birch, cherry

PHOTO BY REGGIE MORROW

Gary Upton

Alter Cabinet | 2006

66 X 31 X 16½ INCHES (167.6 X 78.7 X 41.9 CM)

Ebonized ash with gold fill, spalted maple, hardrock maple, zirocote, selenite crystal, gold paint, tung oil

PHOTOS BY PAUL JEREMIAS

Christoph Neander
Column of Drawers | 1996
58 X 28 X 24 INCHES (147.3 X 71.1 X 61 CM)
White ash, black aniline dye, silver inlay, tung oil varnish
PHOTOS BY JAMES BEARDS

Karen Ernst

Grand Canyon Layers | 2002

30 X 10 X 8 INCHES (76.2 X 25.4 X 20.3 CM) EACH

Cherry, red oak, curly maple, soft maple, silk fabric, Dacron, textured glass, cast bronze, acrylic paint

PHOTOS BY MARK JOHNSTON

Douglas Sigler
Victoria Secrets | 1999
60 X 16 X 16 INCHES (152.4 X 40.6 X 40.6 CM)
Solid pear, ebony inlay, holly
PHOTO BY ARTIST

Adrian Jones

Wing Credenza | 2003

36 X 70 X 18 INCHES (91.4 X 177.8 X 45.7 CM)

Wenge, burr vavona, maple,
boxwood, ebony, lacquer

PHOTO BY ARTIST

Jason Klager

A Showcase of Pear | 2007

45 X 23 X 10 INCHES (114.3 X 58.4 X 25.4 CM)

Steamed pear, East Indian rosewood,
imbuya, brass, oil, varnish

PHOTO BY INGEBORG SUZANNE

Seth Rolland

Blanket Chest | 1995

19 X 41 X 21 INCHES (48.3 X 104.1 X 53.3 CM)

Walnut, cherry, ash

PHOTO BY PAT POLLARD

Kerry Marshall
Shoji Cube Cabinet | 2007
36 X 24 X 24 INCHES (91.4 X 61 X 61 CM)
Madrone, cork veneer, handmade mulberry paper
PHOTO BY ARTIST

Susan Link

Wall Cabinet | 2006

26 X 24 X 6 INCHES (66 X 61 X 15.2 CM)

Cherry-bent laminations, maple,
bent laminations, oil varnish

PHOTO BY ARTIST

Ejler Hjorth-Westh
Tansu Vision | 2009
34 X 54 X 15 INCHES (86.4 X 137.2 X 38.1 CM)
Swiss pear, madrone, gonçalo alves, shellac
PHOTO BY JOHN BIRCHARD

Arnold d'Epagnier

Black-Eyed Susan Sideboard | 2000

36 X 84 X 28 INCHES (91.4 X 213.4 X 71.1 CM)

Curly cherry, ebony, various marquetry
veneers, oil, wax, satin finish, flower bud

PHOTOS BY MICHAEL LATIC

Adam Fisher
Kitchen Produce Stand | 2009
44¹/₂ X 24 X 12³/₄ INCHES (113 X 61 X 32.4 CM)
Maple veneer, cherry, paint, polyurethane, wax
PHOTO BY DEBORAH FISHER

Timothy Coleman

Bow-Front Cabinet | 2005

37 X 50 X 17 INCHES (94 X 127 X 43.2 CM)

Bubinga, walnut, sapele, tung oil, urethane

PHOTO BY DEAN POWELL

Neil Erasmus
Mantis Sideboard | 1992
31½ X 72 X 19⅝ INCHES (80 X 182.9 X 49.8 CM)
Jarrah, jarrah burl, camphor laurel, pigskin suede
PHOTO BY ROBERT YARVEY

Reagan Furqueron

Architectural Cabinet | 2008

32 X 32 X 12 INCHES (81.3 X 81.3 X 30.5 CM)

Ash, graphite

PHOTOS BY JAY YORK

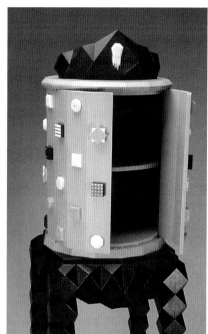

R. Thomas Tedrowe, Jr.
The Jellyfish Queen Cabinet | 2000
70 X 22 X 22 INCHES (177.8 X 55.9 X 55.9 CM)
Ebonized Honduran mahogany, Corian
PHOTOS BY ARTIST

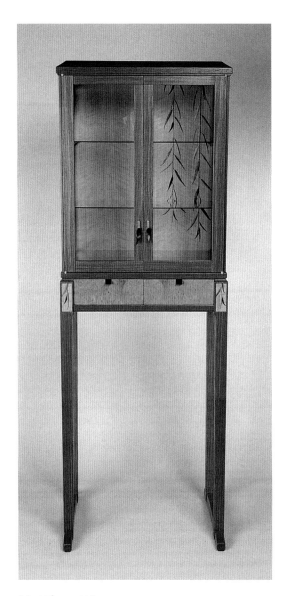

Matthew Werner

Willow Showcase Cabinet | 2002

60 X 20 X 12 INCHES (152.4 X 50.8 X 30.5 CM)

Jarrah, madrone, ebony, brass with patina, maple, glass, various inlay woods, shellac, wax

PHOTO BY PAUL TITANGOS

Brian Sargent
Linen Chest | 2003
32 X 42 X 21 INCHES (81.3 X 106.7 X 53.3 CM)
Madrone burl veneers, walnut, hard
maple, oil varnish, satin lacquer
PHOTO BY CHARLIE FRIEBERG

Richard Oedel

Palm Leaf Book Display Cabinet | 2004

4 X 28 X 20 INCHES (10.2 X 71.1 X 50.8 CM)

White oak, felt, glass

PHOTO BY DEAN POWELL

Thomas Starbuck Stockton
Nightstand | 1993
32 X 35 X 17 INCHES (81.3 X 88.9 X 43.2 CM)
Maple, bird's-eye maple, cherry, walnut, granite
PHOTO BY MATT PRINCE

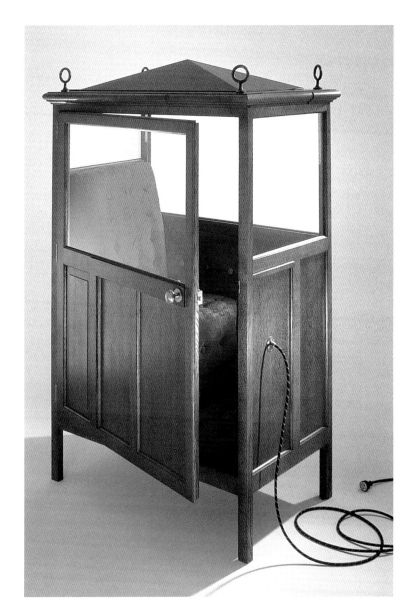

Gord Peteran
Ark | 2001
72 X 48 X 24 INCHES (182.9 X 121.9 X 61 CM)
Oak, oil varnish, glass, velvet, bronze
PHOTO BY DOUG HALL

John R.G. Roth

Surreptitious Return | 2001

69 X 32 X 18 INCHES (175.3 X 81.3 X 45.7 CM)

Cherry, plaster, polystyrene foam,
sheet metal, optic fiber, oil paint

Mats Fogelvik

Fallobelli | 2003

36 X 26 X 12 INCHES (91.4 X 66 X 30.5 CM)

Koa, rosewood, plywood, glass, lacquer, brass

PHOTO BY ROB RATHOWSKI

Michael Puryear
Buffet | 1997
37 X 63 X 19 INCHES (94 X 160 X 48.3 CM)
Bubinga, wenge
PHOTO BY SARAH WELLS

Reagan Furqueron

Wall Wheel Cabinet | 2002

72 X 3¹/₂ X 3¹/₂ INCHES (182.9 X 8.9 X 8.9 CM)

Mahogany, milk paint

PHOTOS BY ARTIST

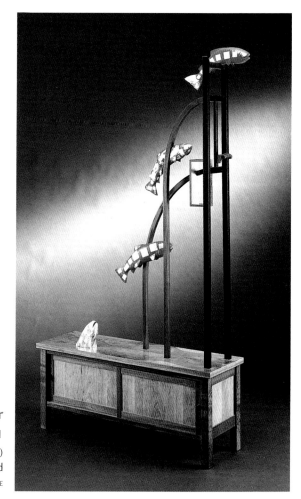

Paul Reiber

Fish Bench | 2001

65 X 48 X 14 INCHES (165.1 X 121.9 X 35.6 CM)

Claro walnut, ash, cherry, gold leaf, pigments, basswood

PHOTO BY JAY ODEE

Kevin Rodel
Glasgow-Style Display Server | 1995
63½ X 57 X 20½ INCHES (161.3 X 144.8 X 52.1 CM)
Fumed white oak, art glass, tiles
PHOTO BY DENNIS GRIGGS

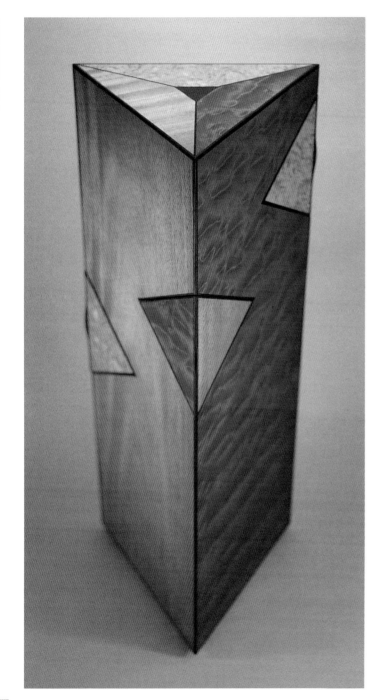

Harold Shapiro
Trident Cabinet | 2005
27 X 11 X 11 INCHES (68.6 X 27.9 X 27.9 CM)
Karelian birch burl, moabi and sapele veneers, Baltic birch ply, ebony, maple, purpleheart, Danish oil, varnish
PHOTOS BY ARTIST

Jim Crampton
Untitled | 2006
25 X 18½ X 7 INCHES (63.5 X 47 X 17.8 CM)
Stained oak, antique metal doors, Chinese
brass handles, polyurethane finish
PHOTO BY ARTIST

Timothy Coleman

So Sweet | 2005

43 X 26 X 12 INCHES (109.2 X 66 X 30.5 CM)

Argentine rose cedar, maple, jatoba, shellac

PHOTOS BY BILL TRASLOW

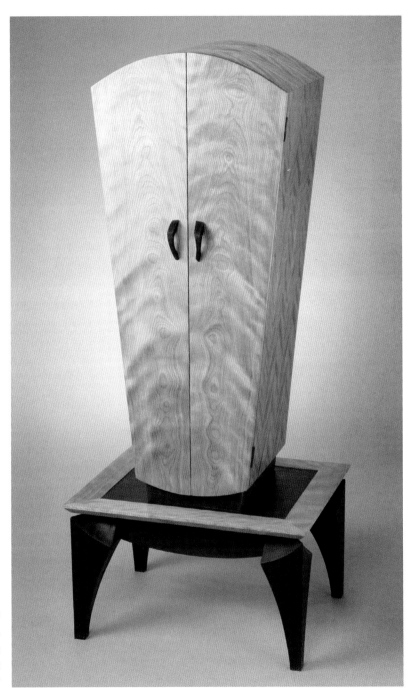

Cale Caboth
Dead Sexy | 2006
54 X 23½ X 19½ INCHES (137.2 X 59.7 X 49.5 CM)
Flamed birch, ebonized walnut

Brian Hubel
Sterling | 2000
48 X 14 X 11 INCHES (121.9 X 35.6 X 27.9 CM)
Claro walnut, ebony
PHOTO BY DON JONES

Adrian Jones

Prism—Collector's Cabinet of 12 Drawers | 1989

60 X 18 X 18 INCHES (152.4 X 45.7 X 45.7 CM)

Macassar ebony, burr thuya, boxwood, ripple sycamore, cedar of Lebanon, English walnut, maple, bronze, lacquer

PHOTOS BY ARTIST

Steve Holman

Self-Portrait Armoire | 2000

84 X 48 X 24 INCHES (213.4 X 121.9 X 61 CM)

Curly maple, mahogany, East Indian rosewood, cherry, purpleheart, aluminum, steel, bronze brazing rod, aniline dyes, gold leaf, lacquer

PHOTOS BY COOK NIELSON

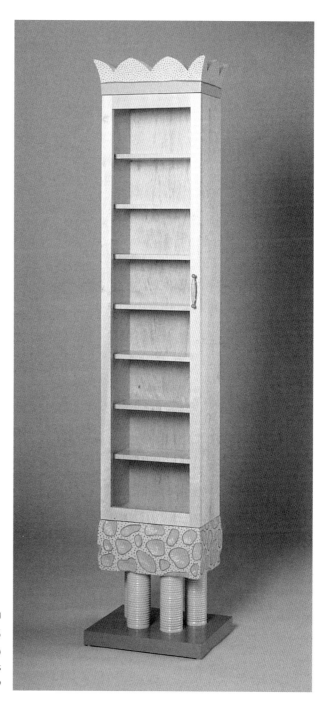

Michael Cullen
King Cabinet | 1996
65 X 14½ X 12 INCHES (165.1 X 36.8 X 30.5 CM)
Wood, maple, paint, glass
PHOTO BY JOHN MCDONALD

Arnold d'Epagnier

Chiffonier | 1986

76 X 48 X 24 INCHES (193 X 121.9 X 61 CM)

Mahogany, Chinese cedar, ebony, pewter, brass, mirrors, aromatic cedar, oil, wax, satin finish

PHOTOS BY BILL KERINS

R. Thomas Tedrowe, Jr.
Chicago Reliquary | 1983
30 X 40 X 20 INCHES (76.2 X 101.6 X 50.8 CM)
Curly maple, Honduran mahogany, Spanish cedar
PHOTOS BY ARTIST

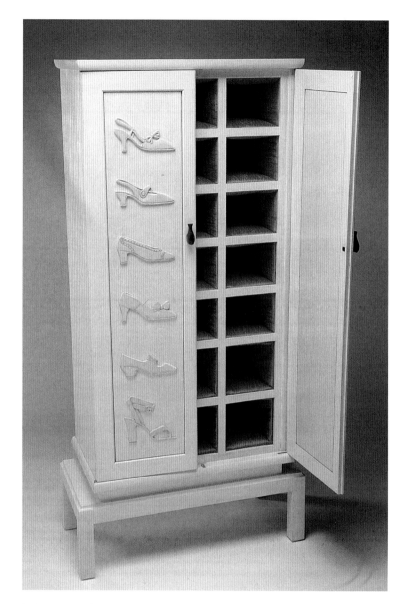

John Houck

Imelda Marcos Shoe Vault | 1997

54 X 32 X 15¼ INCHES (137.2 X 81.3 X 38.7 CM)

Basswood, cocobolo, ebony, raw silk, pigmented shellac

PHOTO BY CLEMENTS/HOWCROFT

Andrew Peklo III

Jewelry Box/Treasure Chest | 1996

72 X 19 X 19 INCHES (182.9 X 48.3 X 48.3 CM)

Curly maple, bloodwood, brass, mirror, leather, stain, varnish

PHOTOS BY ARTIST

Dale Lewis

Take a Bow | 2004

72 X 31 X 20 INCHES (182.9 X 78.7 X 50.8 CM)

Peruvian alder, bubinga, Brazilian cherry, ebonized cherry, holly, lacquer

Jack Glisson
Anniversary | 2007
24 X 23 X 14 INCHES (61 X 58.4 X 35.6 CM)
Sapele, beech, ebony, stained glass, brass, oil varnish
PHOTOS BY ARTIST

Roy Schack

Bronwen's Piece | 2007

35¹/₂ X 59 X 12 INCHES (90.2 X 149.9 X 30.5 CM)

Wenge, New Guinea rosewood, white ash, oil

PHOTO BY FLORIAN GROEHN

Erinco König

Bowed-Front Liquor Cabinet | 2008

42³/₄ X 25¹/₂ X 17¹/₂ INCHES (108.6 X 64.8 X 44.5 CM)

Bird's-eye maple, poplar, brass, ebony, dye, lacquer

PHOTOS BY GORAN BASARIC

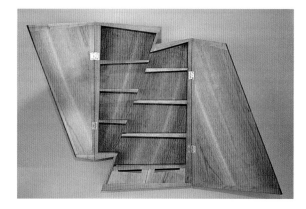

Bibi Harris

Caligari Cabinet | 1993

31 X 49 X 19 INCHES (78.7 X 124.5 X 48.3 CM)

Solid cherry, cherry veneer, brass hinges, oil, varnish

PHOTOS BY JOHN WARNER/WARNER PHOTOGRAPHY

John Thoe
*Cherry Buffet with Carved
Dogwood Bloom Handles* | 1996
34 X 72 X 25 INCHES (86.4 X 182.9 X 63.5 CM)
Cherry, maple
PHOTO BY ARTIST

Peter Handler

Bliss Sideboard | 2004

33 X 48 X 18 INCHES (83.8 X 121.9 X 45.7 CM)

Curly maple, anodized aluminum

PHOTO BY KAREN MAUCH

Toby Winteringham
Untitled | 2003
40 X 78 X 22 INCHES (101.6 X 198.1 X 55.9 CM)
Solid oak, cedar of Lebanon, liming wax
PHOTO BY ARTIST

Scott Sober

Sapele Cabinet and Drawer | 2007

36 X 29 X 17 INCHES (91.4 X 73.7 X 43.2 CM)

Solid sapele, figured sapele veneers, catalyzed satin
lacquer finish, curly maple, medium density fiberboard

PHOTO BY DAVID DITZEL

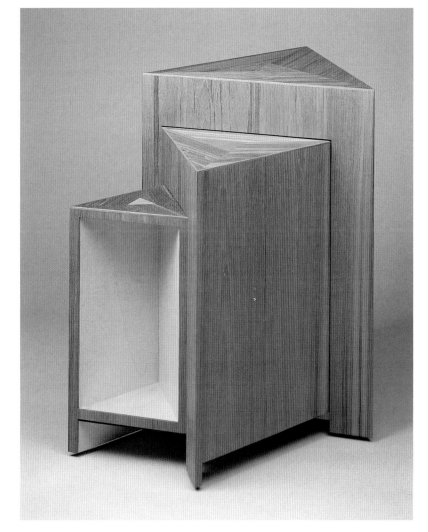

Jennifer Jew
Triangular Tables | 2003
24 X 18 X 18 INCHES (61 X 45.7 X 45.7 CM)
Teak, Alaskan yellow cedar, brass
PHOTOS BY SETH JANOFSKY

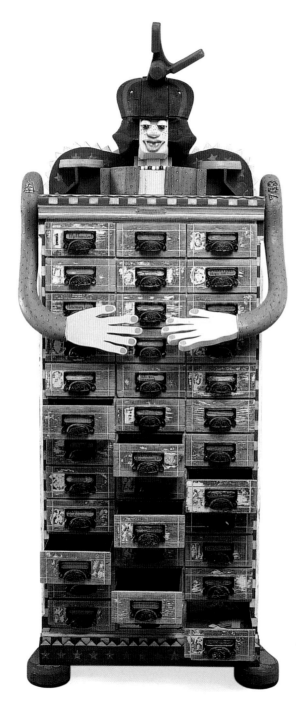

Penny Weinstein
JoAnn's Birthday | 1996
60 X 35 X 15 INCHES (152.4 X 88.9 X 38.1 CM)
Oak, foundry patterns, wood, acrylic paint
PHOTO BY ROBERT RATTNER

Michele Sommer Shapiro

Superman Has a Secret Cabinet 2 | 2008

15½ X 10½ X 3 INCHES (39.4 X 26.7 X 7.6 CM)

Recycled barn board, acrylic paints, aluminum wire,
beads, cut nails, staples, mirror, paper collage,
recycled castings, washers, screws, wire mesh

PHOTO BY HAROLD SHAPIRO

Hugh Montgomery
Hall Entry Cabinetry | 1999
92¼ X 108 X 26¼ INCHES (234.3 X 274.3 X 66.7 CM)
Figured cherry veneers, wenge
PHOTO BY JAMES EWING

Michael Grace
Chest of Drawers | 2005
80 X 48 X 24 INCHES (203.2 X 121.9 X 61 CM)
Douglas fir, purpleheart
PHOTO BY ARTIST

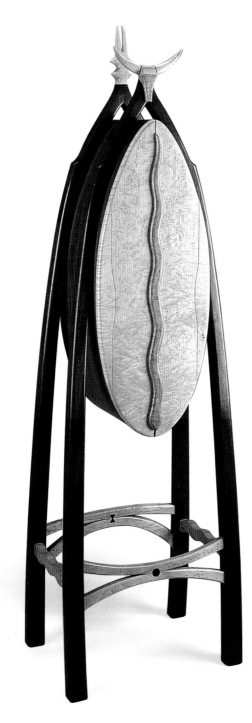

Richard Bronk

Descending Snake Cabinet | 1998

77 X 24 X 17 INCHES (195.6 X 61 X 43.2 CM)

Mahogany, bird's-eye maple, curly maple, wenge, dye, varnish

PHOTOS BY BILL LEMKE

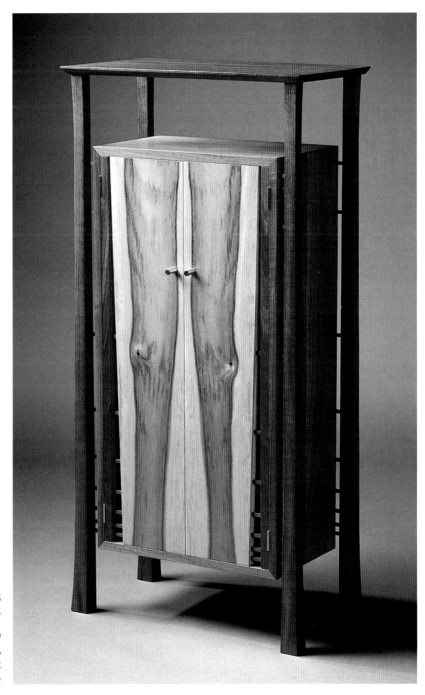

Pam Erasmus

CD's Knees? | 1997

43 X 21 X 11½ INCHES (109.2 X 53.3 X 29.2 CM)

Jarrah, camphor laurel, dyed veneer,
acrylic paint

PHOTO BY ROBERT GARVEY

Keith Clayton
For a Friend | 2001
75 X 27 X 20 INCHES (190.5 X 68.6 X 50.8 CM)
Wenge, African satinwood
PHOTOS BY JERRY W. COX

Bill Bolstad

3 Drawer Jewelry Chest | 2008

11 X 15¹/₂ X 10 INCHES (27.9 X 39.4 X 25.4 CM)

Western maple, walnut, spalted Western maple burl

PHOTO BY DAN KAVITKA

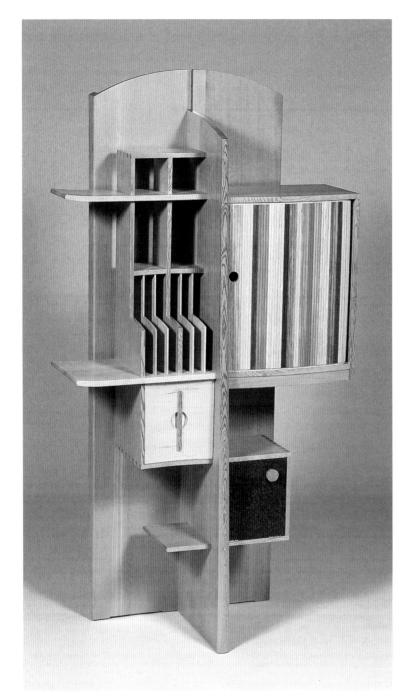

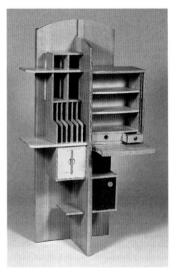

Christoph Neander

Hall Cabinet for Mail | 2002

74 X 40 X 18 INCHES (188 X 101.6 X 45.7 CM)

Douglas fir, maple, acrylic paint,
brass hinges, tung oil varnish

PHOTOS BY DOUG BERRY

Leslie Aguilar

California Cabinet | 2000

10½ X 44½ X 9½ INCHES (26.7 X 113 X 24.1 CM)

California redwood, Douglas fir, shellac, beeswax

PHOTO BY SETH JANOFSKY

Stewart Wurtz

Chestnut Nightstand | 2008

22 X 24 X 14 INCHES (55.9 X 61 X 35.6 CM)

Chestnut, walnut, maple, blackened steel

PHOTO BY TIMOTHY AGUERO

Katrina Tompkins
Burnt Cabin LP Storage | 2008
18 X 28 X 15 INCHES (45.7 X 71.1 X 38.1 CM)
Reclaimed red oak, cast aluminum,
steel, India ink, water-based lacquer
PHOTO BY ARTIST

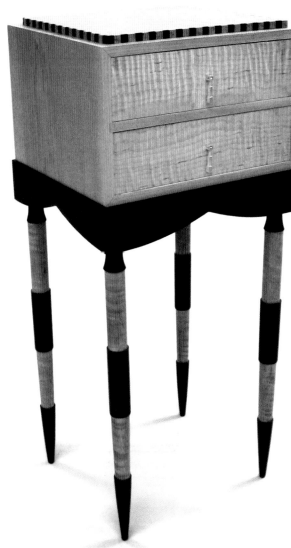

Cosmo Barbaro
Egypt | 2005
29 X 16 X 14 INCHES (73.6 X 40.6 X 35.5 CM)
Maple, ebony, aluminum, milk paint
PHOTO BY ARTIST

Asher Dunn
Untitled | 2008
34 X 54 X 19 INCHES (86.3 X 137.1 X 48.2 CM)
Plywood, oak
PHOTO BY ARTIST

Gary Rawlins
Old Friends—Bookends | 2001
57 X 28½ X 25¼ INCHES (144.8 X 72.4 X 64.1 CM)
Wenge, sugar maple, clear shellac
PHOTOS BY ARTIST

Michael Puryear
Small Chest of Drawers | 1994
36 X 17 X 15 INCHES (91.4 X 43.2 X 38.1 CM)
Mahogany, maple
PHOTO BY SARAH WELLS

Joe Stearns
Kabinett | 2005
55 X 26 X 14 INCHES (139.7 X 66 X 35.6 CM)
American black walnut, curly bubinga,
ash, oil finish
PHOTO BY DAVE SPECKMAN

Scott Grove

Gloria | 2008

42 X 42 X 20 INCHES (106.7 X 106.7 X 50.8 CM)

Pomele sapele, oak, fiberglass reinforced
plastic with copper polychrome finish

PHOTO BY ARTIST

Craig Thibodeau
Lily Cabinet | 2006
42 X 32 X 15 INCHES (106.7 X 81.3 X 38.1 CM)
Wenge, vavona, Honduran mahogany, dyed
poplar, mother-of-pearl, abalone, ebony
PHOTOS BY CRAIG CARLSON

Kevin Rodel

Glasgow Sideboard | 1995

46 X 70 X 22 INCHES (116.8 X 177.8 X 55.9 CM)

Cherry, maple inlay, copper hardware

PHOTO BY DENNIS GRIGGS

Ejler Hjorth-Westh

Sideboard | 2002

38 X 60 X 18 INCHES (96.5 X 152.4 X 45.7 CM)

Swiss pear, bubinga, shellac, varnish

PHOTO BY KEVIN SHEA

Josh Metcalf

Hugo Bookcase | 1985

78 X 78 X 18 INCHES (198.1 X 198.1 X 45.7 CM)

Walnut, hand-forged brass

PHOTO BY ARTIST

Burt Levy

Black-and-White Sideboard | 2005

34 X 84 X 24 INCHES (86.4 X 213.4 X 61 CM)

Wenge, curly English sycamore, figured
maple, ebonized cherry, lacquer finish

PHOTO BY ARTIST

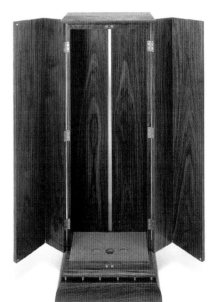

Cathy Adelman

Adelman Family Ark | 2008

49 X 19 X 14 INCHES (124.5 X 48.6 X 35.6 CM)

Walnut, aluminum, cork, oil varnish, wax

ALUMINUM PULLS BY MARVIN JENSEN
PHOTOS BY JERRY MARKATOS

Om Anand

Buddha Box | 1986

13 X 9 X 6 INCHES (33 X 22.9 X 15.2 CM)

Monterey cypress, quilted bigleaf maple,
European pear, shellac, bamboo

PHOTOS BY SEAN SPRAGUE

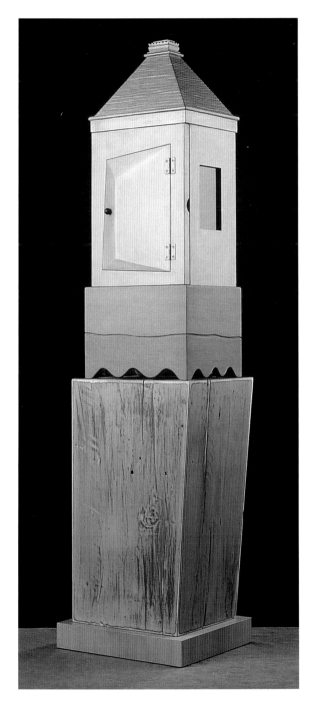

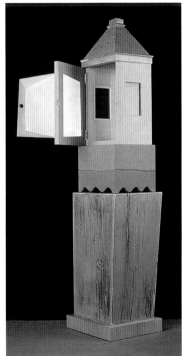

Michael Cullen

The Little Prince | 1999

40 X 9 X 8¹/₂ INCHES (101.6 X 22.9 X 21.6 CM)

Basswood, paint, paper, Port Orford cedar

PHOTOS BY JOHN MCDONALD

Roy Schack

Bon Voyage, Mr. Croker | 2004

31½ X 47 X 14 INCHES (80 X 119.4 X 35.6 CM)

Tasmanian blackwood, white ash, oil

PHOTO BY FLORIAN GROEHN

Glen Guarino

Showtime | 1998

74 X 56 X 23 INCHES (188 X 142.2 X 58.4 CM)

Zebrawood

PHOTO BY RICHARD RUSSO PHOTOGRAPHY, INC.

Jennifer Jew
Jenkins Buffet | 2008
42 X 60 X 14 INCHES (106.7 X 152.4 X 35.6 CM)
Afzelia, maple
PHOTO BY ARTIST

Dale Lewis
I Love You to Pisces | 2002
108 X 48 X 28 INCHES (274.3 X 121.9 X 71.1 CM)
Lacewood, mahogany, maple, Corian
PHOTO BY RALPH ANDERSON

Susan Link

Cherry Buffet | 2008

33 X 46 X 21 INCHES (83.8 X 116.8 X 53.3 CM)

Cherry, bird's-eye maple, oil varnish

PHOTO BY TIM BARNWELL

Arroyo Design

McArthur Credenza | 2009

36 X 60 X 16 INCHES (91.4 X 152.4 X 40.6 CM)

Mesquite, ziricote

PHOTO BY ELLERY BRUMDER

Jay T. Scott

A Box for Diamonds or Old Toothbrushes | 2007

54 X 26 X 15 INCHES (137.2 X 66 X 38.1 CM)

Kwila, bigleaf maple, glass, gold leaf,
brass pulls and hardware, shellac, wax

PHOTO BY AARON BARNA

Jeremy Cox
Grid | 2007
16 X 40 X 14 INCHES (40.6 X 101.6 X 35.6 CM)
Cherry, maple, milk paint, spray enamel
PHOTO BY ARTIST

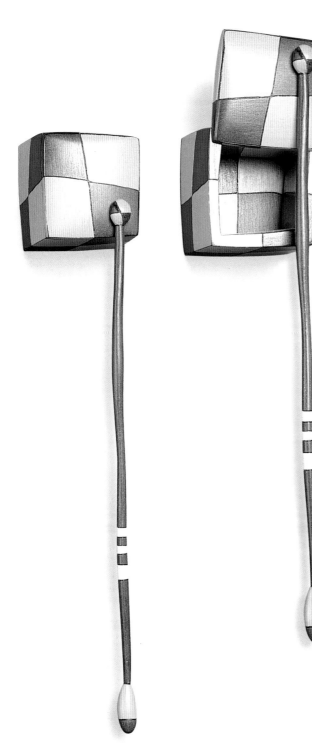

Reagan Furqueron

Checker | 2002

12 X 3½ X 3½ INCHES (30.5 X 8.9 X 8.9 CM)

Mahogany, milk paint

Peter Handler
Hopscotch Cabinet | 2005
52 X 16 X 14 INCHES (132.1 X 40.6 X 35.6 CM)
Oak, anodized aluminum
PHOTO BY KAREN MAUCH

Jennifer Jew

Pear Bookbox | 2004

14 X 18 X 11 INCHES (35.6 X 45.7 X 27.9 CM)

Pear, holly, silver

PHOTOS BY SETH JANOFSKY

Aurelio Bolognesi
Bow-Front Floor Cabinet | 2008
45 X 24 X 16 INCHES (114.3 X 61 X 40.6 CM)
Figured quartersawn cherry, French polish
PHOTO BY BILL TRUSLOW

Trevor Toney

Wall Cabinet | 2004

19³⁄₄ X 12 X 6 INCHES
(50.2 X 30.5 X 15.2 CM)

Mahogany, pear, brass, oil, shellac

Tony Kenway
Buffet | 1998
41 X 48 X 20 INCHES (104.1 X 121.9 X 50.8 CM)
Queensland blackwood, sterling silver knobs
PHOTO BY DAVID YOUNG

Michael Grace

Stereo Cabinet | 1994

50 X 32 X 18 INCHES (127 X 81.2 X 45.7 CM)

English brown oak, cherry, bronze

PHOTO BY ARTIST

Alf Sharp

Block-Front Secretary | 2005

90 X 44 X 22 INCHES (228.6 X 111.7 X 55.8 CM)

Walnut

PHOTO BY JOHN LUCAS

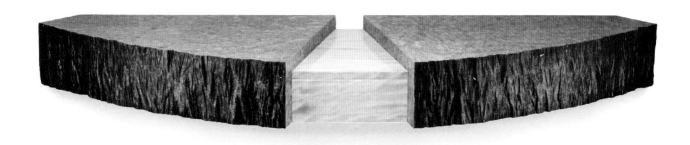

Scott Grove

Slice of Time | 1995

6 X 45 X 12 INCHES (15.2 X 114.3 X 30.4 CM)

Redwood, medium-density fiberboard,
copper polychrome finish

PHOTO BY ARTIST

Alice Porembski

Stereo Cabinet | 1998

30 X 60 X 30 INCHES (76.2 X 152.4 X 76.2 CM)

Lacewood, ebony, birch veneer plywood

PHOTO BY ARTIST

Roger Heitzman
Alcove Credenza | 2007
35 X 68 X 24 INCHES (88.9 X 172.7 X 61 CM)
Mahogany, pomelle sapele, santos
rosewood, polyurethane
PHOTO BY ARTIST

Fatie Atkinson
Cook Cabinet | 2008
48 X 38 X 12 INCHES (121.9 X 96.5 X 30.5 CM)
Bird's-eye maple, sea grass mahogany, ash
PHOTO BY ARTIST

Michael Gloor

Flame-Top Sideboard | 2006

34 X 54 X 22 INCHES (86.4 X 137.2 X 55.9 CM)

Spalted maple, purpleheart, frosted maple veneer, wenge

PHOTO BY DAVID GILSTEIN

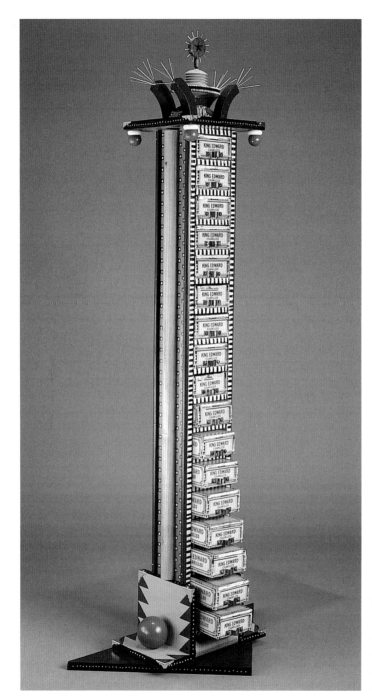

Penny Weinstein

King Edward | 1992

60 X 24 X 20 INCHES (152.4 X 61 X 50.8 CM)

Cigar boxes, found wood and
metal objects, acrylic paint

PHOTO BY ROBERT RATTNER

Frederick Puksta
Father's Time: Cabinet on a Stand | 2007
74 X 19 X 10 INCHES (188 X 48.3 X 25.4 CM)
Zebrawood, ebonized mahogany, paint, electric movement
PHOTO BY JEFFREY STOWELL

Christoph Neander

Sideboard | 2004

35 X 64 X 18 INCHES (88.9 X 162.6 X 45.7 CM)

Curly cherry, Alaskan yellow cedar,
handmade paper, tung oil varnish

PHOTO BY JAMES HART

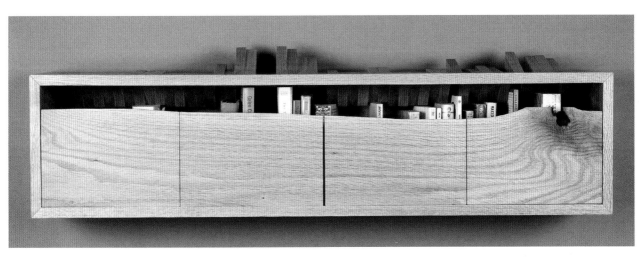

Tony Nguyên

Mimicry | 2007

10 X 42 X 10 INCHES (25.4 X 106.7 X 25.4 CM)

Red oak

PHOTO BY SCAD

Dale Broholm
She's Not Here Anymore Cabinet | 2005
12 X 12 X 8 INCHES (30.4 X 30.4 X 20.3 CM)
Cherry, boxwood, glass, milk paint
PHOTO BY POWELL PHOTOGRAPHY

Brian Paul Kolakowski

I'm Sorry, I Won't Do It Again | 2009

16 X 14 X 11 INCHES (40.6 X 35.6 X 27.9 CM)

Maple, lacquer, razorblade

PHOTO BY ARTIST
DEDICATED TO MARK BECKER AND JEFF SUTA

About the Juror

I've been working with wood for 35 years and feel a great deal of gratitude for the support I received from others. My training began in the night school of the University of the Arts in Philadelphia, where Helmut Gerson taught students how to sharpen a chisel in two minutes. A challenging 16-month apprenticeship with Karl Seemuller and Joyce and Edgar Anderson at the Peters Valley Craft Center in Layton, New Jersey, soon followed, made possible with the assistance of Dan Jackson and Vinton and Eleanor Coes.

In the 1970s, with my late wife, Carolyn Grew-Sheridan, I started working in a tiny corner of a shared shop in San Francisco. I showed my pieces at craft festivals and lived frugally so that I could afford to buy tools. Along the way, I taught classes at an array of schools, and several understanding editors shaped my rough drafts into coherent articles for the woodworking press. Today I belong to The Furniture Society and teach at the Academy of Art University in San Francisco. Carolyn and I both are featured artists in Lark Books' *500 Tables* and *500 Chairs*.

— **John Grew Sheridan** (John's work with Carolyn Grew-Sheridan is featured on this page)

Wes' Cabinet | 1993

Credenza | 1996

Acknowledgments

Esteemed furniture maker and woodworker John Grew Sheridan brought discernment, dedication, and good humor to his role as juror. Thank you, John, for your work and your support of this project.

Our team here at Lark Books also displayed its usual commitment to excellence. Julie Hale, Dawn Dillingham, Wolf Hoelscher, and Larry Shea did wonderful work editorially. Designer Matt Shay laid out the book with intelligence and care, and Kathy Holmes, Carol Morse, and Shannon Yokeley offered invaluable efforts in our art department.

This book is the third one in a furniture-making sequence, and I want to thank Craig Nutt and Andrew Glasgow, the jurors for *500 Chairs* and *500 Tables*, respectively, for their enthusiastic contributions to those terrific titles.

Most of all, of course, my deep appreciation goes to the brilliant, innovative furniture makers featured in the book, for their generosity in sharing these beautiful images of their craftsmanship.

— **Ray Hemachandra, senior editor**

Contributing Artists

A

Adelman, Cathy Malibu, California 387

Aguilar, Leslie Oakland, California 375

Aldridge, Chad Lafayette, Louisiana 179

Allaire, Dan Scottsdale, Arizona 119

Allen, Jacque Asheville, North Carolina 30, 87, 116

Allen, Nick Chichester, West Sussex, England 316

Allen, W. Douglas Baton Rouge, Louisiana 112

Anand, Om Santa Cruz, California 181, 388

Anderson, Jennifer San Diego, California 139

Annels, Ross Cooroy, Queensland, Australia 252

Arms, Isaac Bozeman, Montana 80, 261

Arntzen, Arnt Vancouver, British Columbia, Canada 13, 172

Arroyo Design Tucson, Arizona 395

Atkinson, Fatie Clyde, North Carolina 408

Atwood, Christopher Clifton, Virginia 29

B

Baier, Fred Pewsey, England 61, 125

Baines, Paul Bowdoinham, Maine 171

Barbaro, Cosmo Murray, Kentucky 162, 378

Barrand, Bill Glendale, Arizona 186

Barrett, Neal Rochester, New York 154

Barton, Kevin-Louis San Francisco, California 253

Behling, Erin Dace Louisville, Kentucky 77

Beland, George Portsmouth, New Hampshire 178

Bennett, Gary Knox Oakland, California 76

Bishoff, Bonnie Gloucester, Massachusetts 74

Bledsoe, Denise Temecula, California 58

Bolognesi, Aurelio Hardwick, Massachusetts 401

Bolstad, Bill Jefferson, Oregon 373

Bonnell, Julia Burlington, Ontario, Canada 169

Bossert, Anne Fort Collins, Colorado 49

Boston, Mark Indianapolis, Indiana 238

Boykin, Dave Denver, Colorado 35, 129

Brasseaux, Don Breaux Bridge, Louisiana 218

Breau, Jacques Blackland, New Brunswick, Canada 243

Brinton, Bobby San Francisco, California 190

Britton, Eric Grand Rapids, Michigan 239

Broholm, Dale Wellesley, Massachusetts 414

Bronk, Richard Plymouth, Wisconsin 370

Brown, Gareth Adelaide, South Australia, Australia 146

Bullens, Shaun Providence, Rhode Island 121

Byers, John Eric Newfield, New York 27

C

Caboth, Cale Mt. Pleasant, Iowa 27, 347

Cadman, Arthur Blaenavon, Gwent, Wales 51

Cadman, Rachel Blaenavon, Gwent, Wales 51

Calhoun, Tom Maui, Hawaii 207

Campbell, Graham Smithville, Tennessee 269

Capicik, Kyle Indianapolis, Indiana 160

Chalfant, Derek Elmira, New York 199

Chandler, Nicholas Seville, Spain 289

Christenson, Tom Bakersfield, California 258

Christie, Megan Mundijong, Western Australia 128

Clayton, Keith Chicago, Illinois 372

Coleman, Timothy Shelburne Falls, Massachusetts 306, 330, 346

Cox, Jeremy Philadelphia, Pennsylvania 397

Crampton, Jim Searsmont, Maine 345

Cullen, Michael Petaluma, California 12, 302, 351, 389

D

D'Agnone, Nicola Rouleau, Saskatchewan, Canada 153

d'Epagnier, Arnold Colesville, Maryland 133, 328, 352

Daggett, Barry Northampton, Massachusetts 291

Davidson, Kate Evansville, Indiana 124

De Jong, Frank Toronto, Ontario, Canada 299

Dehner, Justin Savannah, Georgia 237

Del Guidice, Mark Norwood, Massachusetts 22, 144

Dellert, Peter Holyoke, Massachusetts 134, 194

DeLonga, Heather Belleville, Illinois 283

Doan, Jonny San Francisco, California 26

Doig, Trevor Salmo, British Columbia, Canada 188

Doppelt, Kenneth Roslyn Heights, New York 295

Downes, Patrick Griffin Saco, Maine 251

Dunn, Asher Pawtucket, Rhode Island 379

During, Stefan Texel, Holland 259

E

Erasmus, Neil Pickering Brook, Western Australia, Australia 265, 331

Erasmus, Pam Pickering Brook, Western Australia, Australia 371

Ernst, Karen Edinboro, Pennsylvania 176, 320

Esworthy, James Vancouver, British Columbia, Canada 163

F

Factor, Ian Bowral, New South Wales, Australia 301

Farnsworth, Dustin Grand Rapids, Michigan 239, 257

Favero, Sean Dixon, California 232

Fedarko, Aaron Camden, Maine 67

Fernandez, Juan Carlos Sechelt, British Columbia, Canada 246, 298

Fish, Marc Seaford, East Sussex, England 219, 234

Fisher, Adam Stony Brook, New York 329

Fleet, Kyle Byron Center, Michigan 151

Fleming, Shaun Haiku, Hawaii 53, 206, 312

Fogelvik, Mats Makawau, Hawaii 62, 340

French, Adrian Columbus, Ohio 280, 297

Furqueron, Reagan Yarmouth, Maine 90, 100, 332, 342, 398

G

Gale, Russell Franklin, North Carolina 254

Gallagher, John Sydney, New South Wales, Australia 37

Garbus, Arcisan (Bill) New Canaan, Connecticut 45

Gaston, Blaise Earlysville, Virginia 103, 138

Gates, David London, England 24

Gerner, Anton Hawthorn, Victoria, Australia 59

Giffin, Rhea Coeur d' Alene, Idaho 164

Glendinning, John Montreal, Quebec, Canada 39

Glisson, Jack Creedmoor, North Carolina 357

Gloor, Michael Peace Dale, Rhode Island 14, 409

Godfrey, Lord Vancouver, British Columbia, Canada 263

Goldberg, Jenna Providence, Rhode Island 44, 91

Goldenberg, David San Francisco, California 122

Gompf, Floyd Union Pier, Michigan 112

Goodman, Jordan Chicago, Illinois 85, 191

Goodman, Rebecca San Diego, California 78

Gowdy, Duncan Worcester, Massachusetts 110, 130, 142